Voting Rights and Minority Representation

Redistricting, 1992- 2002

Edited by David A. Bositis

Joint Center for Political and Economic Studies®
Washington, DC

University Press of America,® Inc.
Lanham . Boulder . New York . Toronto . Oxford

The Joint Center for Political and Economic Studies informs and illuminates the nation's major public policy debates through research, analysis, and information dissemination in order to: improve the socioeconomic status of black Americans and other minorities; expand their effective participation in the political and public policy arenas; and promote communications and relationships across racial and ethnic lines to strengthen the nation's pluralistic society.

1090 Vermont Avenue, NW, Suite 1100, Washington, DC 20005
www.jointcenter.org

Co-published by arrangement with the Joint Center for Political and Economic Studies, Inc.

University Press of America,® Inc.
4501 Forbes Boulevard, Suite 200
Lanham, Maryland 20706

PO Box 317
Oxford, OX2 9RU, UK

Printed in the United States of America.

British Library Cataloging in Publication Information Available
Library of Congress Control Number: 2004112641
ISBN-13: 978-0-7618-3043-6 (paperback : alk. paper)
ISBN-10: 0-7618-3043-X (paperback : alk. paper)

™ The paper used in this publication meets the minimum requirements of American National Standard for Information Sciences—Permanence of Paper for Printed Library Materials, ANSI Z39.48—1984

Contents

List of Figures and Tables

Figures

Tables

Foreword

Minority representation was greatly advanced following the 1990 round of congressional redistricting, with the creation of almost 20 new majority-minority districts in the U.S. House, and almost 100 such districts in the state legislatures. Those districts subsequently faced legal challenge when the U.S. Supreme Court issued its *Shaw* v. *Reno* decision in 1993. Minority voting rights supporters spent the better part of the 1990s fighting off Shaw-type challenges, and with the Easley decision in 2000, it could be said they had largely succeeded. However, the challenges that have come with the new century have made the Shaw cases seem like distant skirmishes in an on-going conflict. The voting rights struggle is, after all, a fight that is never finished.

The 2000 redistricting cycle produced few gains for blacks and Hispanics. Further, changes in partisan control in several state legislatures minimized the input of minority legislators, and Democrats generally, in redistricting decisions. Several states, including Michigan, Pennsylvania, and Ohio, produced new maps with many fewer Democratic or swing districts, contributing to the continuing Republican dominance of the U.S. House of Representatives.

The Georgia legislature's redistricting produced divisions within the African American community that were hitherto rare. With the Democrats in control of the process, and the Georgia Legislative Black Caucus a full partner in the deliberations, the Democratic majority produced a new map to enhance Democrats' prospects in the new districts. While the Democrats did not succeed in the 2002 elections as well as they had hoped, the only new district in the country electing a black representative to Congress was in Georgia.

The redistricting of Georgia's state senate, though, provoked a legal challenge that split the civil rights community. Several black civil rights leaders—including the Reverend Joseph P. Lowery—joined Republican Governor Sonny Purdue in raising a vote-dilution challenge (under the Voting Rights Act) against the new map. Opposing them were the state's Democratic Party and most of the Georgia Legislative Black Caucus. The case, *Georgia* v. *Ashcroft*, reached the U.S. Supreme Court, where the map was defended by Georgia's black Attorney General Thurbert Baker. In a 5-4 decision, the map was upheld. Justice Sandra Day O'Connor wrote the opinion, in which she gave significant weight to the fact that the black legislators in Georgia supported the new plan.

Additional major challenges for voting rights advocates occurred in Colorado and Texas, where Republicans, newly in control of state government, decided to redraft their Congressional district plans in order to improve Republican prospects. In Texas, after the governor called a special session of the legislature for redistricting, all of the Democrats in the lower house crossed the border to Oklahoma in order to prevent a quorum and therefore block any changes to the existing map. After failing in the first session, the governor called a second session, upon which all of the Democratic senators traveled to New Mexico, again preventing a quorum. A new plan was eventually passed in a third special session. As of this writing, that plan is being litigated in Texas state court.

A similar redistricting effort by Republicans in Colorado failed when it was struck down by the Colorado Supreme Court in *Salazar* v. *Davidson*. The Colorado court ruled that the state constitution permits legislative districting only once a decade. The sometimes bitter partisan conflicts over redistricting have provoked judicial scrutiny for the first time in many years. During the 2003-2004 term, the U.S. Supreme Court has heard a case from Pennsylvania examining the limits of partisan redistricting. The decision in *Vieth* v. *Jubelirer* is expected by the end of the 2003-2004 term.

Throughout its history, the Joint Center for Political and Economic Studies has called attention to the importance of the redistricting process for minority representation. To help those who share these concerns, and to understand the first redistricting process of the twenty-first century, the Joint Center convened a one-day conference entitled "Redistricting, 1992-2002: Voting Rights and Minority Representation." The May 2002 conference brought together many of the nation's most influential figures in the voting-rights and redistricting community. On the panels and in the audience were some of the most prominent voting-rights litigators, black and Hispanic scholars and political activists, journalists, and redistricting experts in the country. The luncheon speakers, Christopher Edley, Jr. (founding codirector of the Civil Rights Project at Harvard) and Maria Echaveste (former deputy chief of staff for President Clinton and cofounder of Nueva Vista Group, LLC), highlighted the theme of the conference—minority representation.

The Joint Center conference commenced with a tribute to the late Frank Parker, an important and much missed defender of minority voting rights. Frank had a long association with the Joint Center, and former Joint Center vice president Milton Morris recounted Frank's time with us. Frank's family, friends, and colleagues also reminisced about his long and distinguished career.

The six major papers presented at the conference form the core of this volume. It has been enriched by the inclusion of an introductory commentary by one of the conference's discussants. This volume has been made possible by the generous support of the Ford and Joyce foundations, and the efforts of its editor, David A. Bositis. Dr. Bositis is a senior research associate at the Joint Center and a nationally renowned expert in the area of redistricting. We hope that the information and analysis presented in this volume contribute to future enhancements of voting rights and minority representation.

Eddie N. Williams
President
Joint Center for Political and Economic Studies

1. Introduction

Advancing Minority Voting Rights: How Do We Get From Here to There?

Anita Earls

This is a crucial time for minority voters and for voting rights advocates. The country is dealing with the effects of the Supreme Court's erosion of the Voting Rights Act's[1] protections, preparing for the struggle to keep Section 5 of the Act in place in 2007,[2] and still reeling from the extraordinary events of the November 2000 presidential election, particularly the disenfranchisement of thousands of black voters.[3] If we who are voting rights advocates are to set the agenda of public discourse, influence future legislative enactments, and shape evolving legal doctrine in this area, we need to have a clear vision of the path ahead. As we stand at this crossroads in the evolution of the very institutions that make democratic participation possible, our key task is to determine which of several avenues we should take. The views presented in each of the chapters of this book indicate that we intuitively share an idea of where we ought to be going but not on how we should get there.

Stated broadly, the ultimate goal of voting rights advocacy is to guarantee that all citizens of every race have an equal opportunity to vote and to participate in the political process. In the redistricting context, equal opportunity is frequently measured by assessing whether minority voters have the ability to elect candidates of their choice to public office. Laughlin McDonald (Chapter 2), for example, writes about how to achieve "effective minority political participation and black office holding," while Lisa Handley (Chapter 4) examines a model that "can be used to determine whether a proposed redistricting plan, and more specifically, whether certain minority districts within the proposed plan, offer minority voters an opportunity to elect candidates of choice." Similarly, Leo Estrada (Chapter 5) primarily discusses Latino political power in terms of Latino office-holding and Latino participation in political party leadership.

While it is true, as David Lublin points out (chapter 7), that African American voters almost always choose African American candidates when given the opportunity to choose between them and non-black candidates, it is important to remember that the basic guarantee of equal political rights for all citizens, regardless of their skin color, involves the voter's equal opportunity to participate and not any particular candidate's right to be elected. The Voting Rights Act is not an affirmative action plan for black, Latino or Asian candidates; it is a basic application of the one-person, one-vote principle, made necessary by the distorting effects of past and present racial discrimination. Hence, the relevant question initially is whether minority voters can elect the individual they prefer to represent them.

One significant controversy that surfaced in the conference on which this book is based is whether minority voters ever can be said to have an equal opportunity to elect a candidate of their choice in a district where the minority population is less than 50 percent of the total population. The debate is a complex one. It involves our concepts of what equal opportunity means in the political context, what it means to be a "preferred candidate" of a particular community, and our understanding of the nature of meaningful political representation. These are questions of political philosophy and social science; the legal doctrines merely reflect and embody underlying assumptions that are made about the requirements of democratic government.[4] The two positions on this issue can be simplified and summarized as follows.

What might be termed a traditional view holds that African American or other minority voters only can have an equal opportunity to elect a candidate of their choice in a jurisdiction that is at least 50 percent African American in voting-age population. According to this point of view, there is no equality of opportunity when African American voters can only elect a candidate of their choice by forming coalitions with white voters to support a particular candidate and white voters do not need similar coalitions with black voters in order to elect their candidate of choice. An illustrative district to prove liability under Section 2 of the Voting Rights Act must be less than 50 percent minority in voting-age population in order to demonstrate that vote dilution has occurred, and any district ultimately drawn to remedy or avoid that dilution of minority voting strength must be at least 50 percent minority. In this view, the goal is to structure the election system so that any candidate who is chosen and supported by the entire minority community will win election.

The alternative view is that minority voters can have an equal opportunity to elect candidates of choice in districts that are less than 50 percent minority when there are sufficient white voters who are willing to vote for the candidate preferred by minority voters. In this view, districts that avoid diluting the votes of minority voters can be something less than 50 percent minority. Such districts are sufficient to establish liability under Section 2 of the Voting Rights Act and can be sufficient to avoid or remedy vote dilution.[5] This view opens the door to political empowerment of minority communities when compactness or other concerns make it difficult to draw a 50 percent minority district. It also requires a more detailed explanation of what it means to be a "candidate of choice" of minority voters and carries the danger of permitting the erosion of majority-minority districts to a point where minority-preferred candidates can no longer be elected.

This debate is not one that is easily resolved. Solutions, however, are apparent when viewing the issue at a more focused level, as detailed in this book. Fortunately, we can move forward with vigorous voting rights advocacy and debate the controversies in political philosophy in our spare time. These papers show us the way.

Laughlin McDonald appropriately starts with a quick review of how the Voting Rights Act and the development of legal doctrines through subsequent legislation and court opinions brought about greater black political participation through the use of majority-minority districts. The early 1990s brought a severe white backlash led by Justice O'Connor's opinion for the Court in *Shaw v. Reno.*[6] McDonald's assessment is that while *Shaw v. Reno* and subsequent cases have had an impact, "the worst predictions that it would systematically roll back the gains in minority office holding have not come to pass."

Interestingly, McDonald finds that one reason for this is the increased influence of black elected officials. Having black elected officials in office and at the table during redistricting debates makes it easier to maintain election structures that allow black voters a fair chance at electing candidates of their choice. It would certainly be useful to know how the debate surrounding other issues, and not just issues traditionally thought of as race issues, has been affected by having black elected officials in Congress, state legislatures, and local government. This would help us counter the argument that it is not necessary to have black voters' candidate of choice elected in order to have those voters' concerns addressed.

Some argue that black voters can be adequately represented by candidates whose election they merely influence rather than control. One of the more memorable instances of that argument occurred during the oral argument in *Shaw v. Hunt*,[7] when Justice Antonin Scalia leaned forward and asked Julius Chambers, who was arguing on behalf of black voters from North Carolina, what it meant to be a candidate of choice of the black community. This exchange demonstrates the dangers of advocating for influence districts and why the traditional view continues to appear the safest road to take. The colloquy is instructive even without hearing the extreme skepticism in Justice Scalia's voice and the barely controlled anger in Mr. Chambers' voice:

> SCALIA: Mr. Chambers, many people think that black people can have a greater voice when they are close to a majority, or at least a substantial minority in a lot of districts, rather than a majority in one or two districts. Indeed, the charge is made that it is very much in the political interests of some people to aggregate all blacks into one or two districts so that the rest of the districts can ignore their interests.
>
> I don't—you know, I am in total sympathy with the objective that you're urging upon us, but it certainly isn't clear as a matter of principle or logic that this is the only way to achieve that objective. Indeed, there are many who think that this is moving in precisely the wrong direction, that its net effect is to reduce the opportunity of blacks to have their interests taken into account.
>
> I frankly don't know what the answer is, but I certainly can't agree with you that this is the only way to achieve it.
>
> MR. CHAMBERS: I understand that, your Honor. We had a district in North Carolina that provided—we thought—an opportunity, with 42 percent black votes. Because of racially polarized voting we elect a candidate of choice.

> SCALIA: What does that mean, you couldn't elect a candidate of choice? Is it clear that the candidate you elected ignored the interests of black people, or is it just that he was not black?
>
> MR. CHAMBERS: It's because the candidate was not the representative of choice for African Americans in North Carolina.
>
> SCALIA: I don't know what that means. I don't know what that means.
>
> MR. CHAMBERS: It means, your Honor, the same thing it would mean for you if you didn't have a voice in the election of your representative. We've gone through periods where we know, through the legislation that's been passed in Congress, where the interests of black people haven't been represented.[8]

What this abbreviated discussion illustrates is that it is all too easy to undermine the legitimate claims of minority communities for effective political participation by suggesting that minority voters should be satisfied with "influencing" who is elected rather than seeking to control the election. One way to counter this danger is to focus on the difference between minority voters' being able to elect their chosen candidate and minority voters' influencing which of two or more candidates of choice of white voters will be elected.[9] In concrete terms, returning to a North Carolina example, it is the difference between being able to elect Harvey Gantt to the U.S. Senate and influencing whether Elizabeth Dole or Erskine Bowles is elected to the Senate. It is certainly the perception among minority voters, based on their voting patterns, that the former is preferable to the latter.[10] More important, minority voters cannot be said to have an equal opportunity to participate if they are limited to influencing which of white voters' candidates of choice will be elected, while white voters have the opportunity to elect their candidate of choice every time.

McDonald concludes by taking a look at two significant features of the current legal rules governing redistricting—that legislatures or others who are drawing redistricting plans must be faithful to the Voting Rights Act while being careful to avoid allowing race to predominate in the redistricting process, and that partisan gerrymandering, in contrast, can proceed with a legal "green light."

David Bositis's work (Chapter 3) provides a vital documentary of the current landscape. He examines voting patterns in the South and concludes that "although it has declined somewhat in recent years, racially polarized voting continues to be a defining condition of Southern politics." He evaluates two of the main criticisms of majority-minority districts and then looks at the impact of majority-minority districts on the partisan balance in the South. He concludes by considering whether such districts are necessary to give minority voters an equal opportunity to elect candidates of choice. Both McDonald and Bositis conclude that at this point the political process is not "color-blind." They agree that majority-minority districts are still needed in order to permit fair electoral opportunities for minority voters because of the continuing practice of racially polarized voting. At first sight, Lisa Handley's thesis may seem to be at odds with this view. She sets out to demonstrate that it is possible, using the model she and others have developed, to estimate the percentage of a district's population that must be black to enable that district's black voters to elect their preferred candidate. She argues that the proper interpretation of the Voting Rights Act requires focus on "actual election outcomes, not on rigid demographic 'cutoff lines' such as 50 percent minority population, to determine the minority percentage necessary to provide minority voters with an opportunity to elect minority-preferred candidates."

It is possible to harmonize Handley's approach with that of the other two writers through a rule that posits: Where polarized voting exists sufficient to deny black voters an equal opportunity to elect candidates of choice, draw majority-black districts if possible, do not pack minority voters in districts with overwhelming black percentages, and draw districts that are electable for the candidates of choice of black voters, using the Handley model, when it is not possible to reach something greater than a 50 percent majority of black voters. A functional, case-specific analysis of electoral opportunities for minority voters does not necessarily require abandoning the majority-minority district as a vehicle for minority political participation.

McDonald has correctly identified the current trend of Republicans' seeking to pack black voters into as few districts as possible, under the guise of compliance with Section 2 or Section 5 of the Voting Rights Act.[11] Conversely, Democrats have tried to use minority voters to their own advantage by spreading them out among as many districts as possible, reducing majority-black districts to under 50 percent black. Interestingly, in the 1990s round of redistricting, the Republicans followed the same strategy they are following now, but because there were so few majority-minority districts in 1990, particularly at the Congressional level but also at the state legislative level, the packing strategy actually aligned Republicans with the interests of black voters. Concentrating black voters in the 1990s round of redistricting meant creating opportunities where none existed before. Now, against a backdrop of majority-minority districts in existence for some time, the Republicans' strategy has put them at odds with the interests of minority voters. Concentrating black voters this time around meant diminishing their opportunities and decreasing the number of majority-minority districts.

In both decades, the tension between creating as many solid Democratic districts as possible and yet also giving minority voters fair representation put the Democratic party in potential conflict with those voters. This perennial conflict, created precisely because black voters do see themselves as sharing similar interests and vote accordingly, was resolved in a variety of ways. This time around, we were trying to preserve what we have, with minority elected officials having a role in the process. In the 1990s, we were trying to create new opportunities with the amended Voting Rights Act, as interpreted by *Thornburg v. Gingles*,[12] providing a formidable legal avenue for redress if the enacted plans ended up diluting minority voting strength.

It should be noted that this analysis applies primarily to the experience of black voters in the South, in states covered by Section 5 of the Voting Rights Act,[13] and to a lesser degree to black voters in northern urban areas. The experience for other minority groups, including Hispanic voters and Native American voters, has been different. Their progress in achieving fair representation has been somewhat slower in the past, but it was more significant than that of black voters in the 2000 round of redistricting.

When all election districts are finally redrawn nationwide, it is most likely that more Hispanic voters (both as a percentage and in absolute numbers) will find themselves in majority-Hispanic districts than was the case in the 1990s. In contrast, it is likely that fewer African American voters will be able to vote in majority-black districts. We know that at the congressional level, for example, in 2000 only 35.8 percent of the nation's black voting age population lived in districts represented by Congressional Black Caucus members, while immediately following the 1990s round of redistricting that figure was 42.4 percent. (David Bositis details these numbers in Chapter 3.)

As another measure of this trend, to date the U.S. Department of Justice has objected under Section 5 of the Voting Rights Act to statewide redistricting plans in three states: Arizona, Texas, and Florida.[14] In each state, the basis for the objection was that the redistricting plan in question was retrogressive with regard to Hispanic voters. In the 1990s, many of the Justice Department's objections to statewide plans, including objections to redistricting plans in North Carolina and Georgia, were based on the impact those plans had on the voting strength of black voters.[15]

Laughlin McDonald's work in Montana and other states in the west in recent years has created Native American districts where previously none existed.[16] Although Arizona is covered by Section 5, most of the other western states with large Native American populations are not. Nevertheless, the protections of the Voting Rights Act have been increasingly significant for these populations in recent years.

Another point in McDonald's paper has important implications for the election reform measures that are being considered in state legislatures and in Congress. McDonald reports that for the 10-year period from 1978 to 1988, the United States was a plaintiff in only 105 of the 2,052 voting cases filed in federal court, or about 5 percent of the total cases. All of the other cases were brought by private plaintiffs.[17] There is reason to believe that the data from 1988 to 1998 would show a roughly similar pattern. Judging by past experience, if current election reform measures are to be effective they must allow for private enforcement.

Several interesting questions for further empirical analysis arise from David Bositis's useful study of voting patterns in southern states in the past 10 years. What impact has the creation of majority-minority districts had on the ability to analyze racially polarized voting? There are now very few white vs. black election contests in majority-white jurisdictions. Some courts have corrupted the measurement of racially polarized voting by requiring examination of elections involving only white candidates and giving those election contests equal weight to elections involving white and black candidates.[18] What analytical tools are at our disposal to correct this problem? Can the type of data gathered help reverse another trend in the law that is devastating for Section 2 plaintiffs, namely, courts that from confusion or by design ignore the legislative history of the Voting Rights Act and increasingly require plaintiffs to prove "causation," that is, to prove that discriminatory intent causes racially polarized voting?[19]

All of these questions are relevant to the political participation of Latino voters as well. However, achieving an equal opportunity for Latino voter participation also raises unique issues. These are highlighted by Leo Estrada (Chapter 5) in his examination of how Latinos fared during the 2001 redistricting cycle. Estrada emphasizes four main points in his analysis. First, Latino political influence is not as great as their numbers suggest it should be, because of "demographic denial." Latinos are ignored by elected officials and policy makers because they are seen as a regional minority. The reality is that Latino population growth has extended beyond the border states, as the population disperses in search of jobs in agriculture, food processing, construction, and service industries.

Second, Latino voters did not see their actual voting strength reflected in the newly drawn districts, because state legislators were advised by their lawyers during the redistricting that talking about race could raise the specter of potential *Shaw*-type challenges to the newly enacted redistricting plans. Legislators began to act as though the mere mention of the racial and ethnic demographics of a particular redistricting plan might make it unconstitutional, thus hindering the ability of advocates to discuss what is required to guarantee fair representation.

Third, there are places in the country where redistricting was portrayed as a "zero-sum game" for minorities as a whole. In other words, any gains by Latino voters were viewed as coming only at the expense of black voters. Where this strategy was employed successfully, there were tensions among different racial and ethnic groups. Estrada also notes, however, that in other areas black, Latino, and Asian voters were able to create effective multiracial coalitions, to the benefit of all groups.

Fourth, Latino gains were not as great as they should have been in the redistricting process because legislators viewed the Latino electorate as weak, uninvolved, and not likely to react or retaliate if the process ignored their interests. In fact, this is an extension of the historical practice of redistricting occurring in back rooms, away from the public eye, with the hope and expectation that it would not be a high-profile issue for any constituents.

Estrada concludes that Latinos can only increase their representation over the next decade by challenging non-Latino incumbents. As their numbers continue to increase at higher rates than for any other minority group in the country, and their political mobilization continues to grow using means such as the increasingly popular Spanish-language media, Latinos will have greater political influence and increased representation.

Bob Holmes (Chapter 6) and David Lublin (Chapter 7)) also analyze redistricting outcomes but from very different vantage points. Their papers both illustrate the practical political struggles over "safe" districts versus "coalition" or "influence" districts, which occurred in the last round of redistricting and are sure to become even more prominent in the years ahead. Holmes is a participant-observer in these matters, a state legislator and member of the Georgia Legislative Black Caucus during some of the most contentious redistricting battles of any over the past 20 years. As he reports, late-night redistricting sessions led to frayed tempers, deadlock, and mutual recriminations. Several years later, Republican state senators filibustering a Democratic-favored plan actually cried on the floor of the Georgia Senate as they talked about the districts. In his experience during the 1990s, opponents of majority-black districts, who had succeeded in dismantling the majority-black districts of Sanford Bishop and Cynthia McKinney by claiming they amounted to racial gerrymandering, argued that "blacks should form biracial coalitions to win election." In that context, "influence" districts are drawn in order to diminish black voting strength.

According to Holmes, politicians also believed that reducing the percentage of black voters in Georgia's legislative districts in the 2001 round of redistricting was necessary in order for white Democrats to win elections in adjacent districts. This fascinating behind-the-scenes account of Georgia's redistricting battles is all the more significant in light of the Supreme Court's 2003 decision in *Georgia v. Ashcroft.*[20] As Holmes explains, Georgia decided to seek preclearance of its redistricting plans under Section 5 of the Voting Rights Act by going to the D.C. District Court rather than submitting them to the Ashcroft Justice Department. When the D.C. Court, following the arguments of the Justice Department, refused to preclear the plan and required the state to increase the black percentage in three state senate districts, Georgia appealed to the Supreme Court. In a five to four decision, the Supreme Court vacated the District Court opinion, ruling that in determining whether the Senate redistricting plan was retrogressive, the Court should also consider the extent to which the plan provides black voters the opportunity to elect candidates of their choice by forming coalitions with other voters "who together will help to achieve the electoral aspirations of the minority group."[21]

In coming to this conclusion, the majority opinion characterizes the options a state legislature has in drawing redistricting plans as the choice between creating a smaller number of safe majority-black districts versus a greater number of districts in which it is highly likely that minority voters will be able to elect candidates of their choice. Reading the Court's philosophical and largely theoretical musings about these options and its benign conclusion that "Section 5 gives States the flexibility to choose one theory of effective representation over the other"[22] conjures up the image of elder statesmen wisely contemplating the best way to ensure that all of Georgia's citizens have an equal opportunity to elect candidates of their choice, and after careful, well-informed deliberations, deciding among competing political philosophies.

The gritty truth that Bob Holmes reveals is not simply bad tempers and tears. His account is replete with the realities of the various "agendas" that rise and fall throughout the redistricting process. In the 2001 round of redistricting, for example, the governor of Georgia wanted to make sure he could continue to have a working Democratic majority in the state legislature. The Speaker was determined that Representative Bob Barr would not continue to represent his home county in Congress; other Democrats were concerned to avoid a plan that would provoke one of the popular Republican members of Congress to seek statewide office, potentially running against Democrat incumbents for the U.S. Senate or the governor's office. In addition, there were agendas involving drawing Congressional districts for potential favorite candidates. In short, redistricting in Georgia was a continuously shifting sea of many currents, large and small, in which the goal of fair representation for black voters played a part, but was also sacrificed for other goals.

Both the Supreme Court opinion and the redistricting process as it actually occurred in Georgia leave a disturbing problem in their wake. They leave us without a firm factual foundation for determining whether the senate districts that the Supreme Court concluded are not retrogressive will, in fact, give black voters the opportunity to elect candidates of their choice or relegate them to simply influencing which of two white-preferred candidates will be elected. As the dissenting justices in *Georgia v. Ashcroft* rightly observed, before a state shifts from majority-minority to coalition districts, under the Section 5 retrogression standard the state has the burden of proving, based on voting behavior data and not simply by showing district population percentages, that nonminority voters will reliably vote along with the minority.[23]

David Lublin (Chapter 7) does base his analysis on voting behavior data. His work has impacted the Supreme Court's development of the law in this area, as it is reflected in the Georgia opinion. Lublin carefully examines the extent to which the creation of majority-black state legislative and congressional districts in the 1990s impacted the partisan shift at the state and federal levels. While he acknowledges that the partisan shift from Democrats to Republicans in the South, in particular, was caused in part by pro-Republican shifts in white voting behavior, his study concludes that the impact of those shifts was exacerbated by the creation of more majority-black districts.

In the northern urban areas, Democratic strength is such that the creation of majority-black districts did not contribute to significant gains or losses in state legislatures or congressional delegations. However, even some of the most carefully drawn maps designed to protect Democrats in the South were vulnerable to small shifts among white voters moving to the Republican Party. In Lublin's words, "Racial redistricting removed the cushion provided by black Democrats against a swing to the GOP among white voters."

In addition, the *Shaw v. Reno* line of cases made it more difficult for Democrats to enact partisan gerrymanders intended to make sure that even when majority-black districts are drawn, Democrats maintain their strength overall.[24] Lublin estimates that because of the creation of majority-black districts, Democrats lost 10 seats in Congress during the 1990s, and from 1990 to 1994 lost 45 seats in state legislatures. Thus, he concludes that the creation of majority-black districts increased the polarization of southern politics by reducing the number of moderate white Democrats and increasing the numbers of liberal black Democrats and conservative white Republicans.

As described by Bob Holmes (Chapter 6), the legislators in the 2001 round of redistricting in Georgia appear to have been aware of the partisan implications of drawing majority-black districts, even without the benefit of Lublin's rigorous analysis. This panel at the conference generated heated debate over questions such as the appropriateness of using the term "racial redistricting," whether there are other reasons that explain Republican gains, what strategies should be followed in light of these observations about partisan voting behavior, and how we can ultimately solve the problem of minority underrepresentation that continues to plague our political process.

The contributors to this book suggest how far we still have to go, and some possible avenues we should follow. They are complementary and remarkably consistent. At the most fundamental and significant level, Handley, Bositis, and

McDonald start from the proposition that black voters, as a group, have distinct political interests and, therefore, a fair democratic election process must give them an opportunity to elect candidates of their choice who can protect and advance those interests at all levels of government. There are now, and always have been, those who do not agree with this proposition.

This book is a fitting tribute to Frank Parker—its chapters catalog the gains that have been made in a decade of voting rights progress that he ushered in by his tireless and devoted advocacy to advance the promise of democracy for all citizens, including black voters in the Mississippi Delta. They also identify the challenges ahead. We only wish that Frank Parker could be here to give us guidance and the benefit of his wisdom and experience as we attempt to move forward. No doubt he would make it seem easy, and we would be better equipped for the journey ahead.

NOTES

1 42 U.S.C. § 1973.

2 The preclearance provisions of Section 5 of the Voting Rights Act will automatically expire in 2007 unless renewed by Congress. See 42 U.S.C. § 1973.

3 This occurred most notoriously in Florida; see, e.g., U.S. Commission on Civil Rights, "Voting Irregularities in Florida During the 2000 Presidential Election," June 2001 at Chapters 1, 2, 5, and 9, where, in addition to the problems with punch card ballots, alleged felons and voters having duplicate registrations in more than one county were erroneously purged from voter rolls prior to the election and not allowed to vote. However, there are estimates that nationwide over 1.2 million voters were disenfranchised in the November 2002 elections and that black voters were disproportionately affected by the problems that occurred in Georgia, California, Illinois Missouri, and elsewhere. See Democratic Investigative Staff, House Committee on the Judiciary, "How to Make Over One Million Votes Disappear: Electoral Sleight of Hand in the 2000 Presidential Election" at 4 and passim, August 20, 2001.

4 In *Georgia v. Ashcroft*, No. 02-182, 2003 U.S. Lexis 5012, June 26, 2003, the Supreme Court issued an opinion in which these two views are described in terms of a state's option to create "safe" districts or to create "coalitional" and "influence" districts. *Georgia*, slip. op. at *36-37. Relying heavily on the work of David Lublin and Lisa Handley, among others, Justice O'Connor, writing for the five to four majority on the Court, noted that "various studies have suggested that the most effective way to maximize minority voting strength may be to create more influence or coalitional districts." Id., at *40. The Court upheld Georgia's voluntary creation of state senate districts that were intended to give black voters an opportunity to elect candidates of their choice even though they are less than 50 percent black in population as non-retrogressive under Section 5 of the Voting Rights Act, 42 U.S.C. § 1973c.

5 Courts have found that when minority candidates can be elected in districts that are less than 50 percent minority, such districts are sufficient to defeat a Section 2 claim; see, e.g., *Vecinos de Barrio Uno v. City of Holyoke*, 72 F. 3d 973, 990-91 (1st Cir. 1995) (holding that the ability to elect a candidate of choice in a district that is 28 percent Hispanic may be sufficient in the totality of circumstances to demonstrate that Hispanic voters have an equal opportunity to elect candidates of choice). However, the corollary, that a claim for vote dilution lies where minorities can elect a candidate of choice in a district that is less than 50 percent minority, has been accepted by some courts and rejected by others. Compare *Armour v. Ohio*, 775 F. Supp. 1044, 1059 (N.D. Ohio 1991) (finding that although the proposed district only had approximately 33 percent black voting age residents, given the voting patterns of both white and black voters, the black community could elect a candidate of their choice in that district; therefore, the failure to draw such a district was vote dilution in violation of Section 2 of the Voting Rights Act), with *McNeil v. Springfield Park Dist.*, 851 F.2d 937, 944-45 (7th Cir. 1988) (rejecting plaintiffs' claim where they were 50.2 percent of the total population of the demonstration district, but not a majority of the voting age population).

6 509 U.S. 620 (1993).

7 517 U.S. 899 (1996).

8 *Shaw v. Hunt*, Nos. 94-923, 94-924, Transcript of Oral Argument at 54-55, December 5, 1995, 1995 U.S. Trans Lexis 117.

9 See *Page v. Bartels*, 144 F. Supp. 2d 346, 359 n.12 (D. N.J. 2001) for another definition of the difference between ability to influence and ability to elect, citing the trial testimony of a noted expert, Dr. Lowen.

10 Surely any identifiable, politically cohesive group of voters would prefer to have an opportunity to elect the candidate who is their first choice for a political office rather than be constrained to choose among candidates selected by another group. Would Republicans be happy to be able to "influence" which candidate from the Democratic party is elected or would they prefer to have the opportunity to elect a Republican candidate?

11 In addition to the Georgia experience that Laughlin documents, similar patterns became the focus of lawsuits in Virginia and elsewhere. See, e.g., *Wilkins v. West*, 571 S.E.2d 100 (Va 2002).

12 478 U.S. 30 (1986).

13 See http://www.usdoj.gov/crt/voting/sec_5/covered.htm for a list of the jurisdictions that are covered by Section 5.

14 The dates of these objections and the text of the objection letters can be found at: http://www.usdoj.gov/crt/voting/sec_5/obj_activ.htm.

15 See, e.g., *Shaw* v. *Reno*, 509 U.S. 620, 635 (1993); *Miller v. Johnson*, 515 U.S. 900, 906-07 (1995).

16 See *Cuthair v. Montezuma-Cortez*, Colorado School Dist., 7 F.Supp. 1152 (D.Colo. 1998).

17 McDonald, supra n. 4 at 9.

18 See, e.g., *Lewis v. Alamance County*, 99 F. 3d 600, 607 (4th Cir. 1996); *Askew v. City* of *Rome*, 127 F.3d 1355, 1373 (11th Cir. 1997).

19 For an example of a court's recognition and rejection of this trend in Section 2 litigation, although in the context of felon disfranchisement rather than redistricting, see *Farrakhan v. Locke*, No. 01-35032, slip op. at 10144, (9th Cir. July 25, 2003).

20 No. 02-182, 2003 U.S. Lexis 5012, June 26, 2003.

21 *Georgia*, slip op. at *38.

22 *Georgia*, slip op. at *39.

23 *Georgia*, slip op. at *58-59.

24 It will be interesting to see what the Supreme Court does in addressing the issue of partisan gerrymandering in the next term, as the Court has agreed to review a case from Pennsylvania that raises the question of what standard should be applied to partisan gerrymandering claims under the equal protection clause. See *Vieth v. Jubelirer*, 188 F. Supp. 2d 532 (M.D. Pa. 2002), prob. juris. noted No. 02-1580, (U.S. June 27, 2003).

2. Redistricting and Voting Rights Issues, 1992-2002: A Legal Analysis

Laughlin McDonald

Many of the discriminatory practices historically used to deny minorities the right to register to vote in the South were finally struck down in the 1960s. Proof of payment of a poll or head tax as a condition for voting in federal elections was banned by the Twenty-Fourth Amendment in 1964. The Voting Rights Act of 1965 abolished literacy tests and other similar requirements for voting, and the following year the U.S. Supreme Court invalidated the poll tax in state elections.[1] All of these reforms, particularly the abolition of literacy tests, greatly increased minority registration.

But as important as registration was, it still did not translate into an ability for minorities to elect candidates of their choice. In majority-white jurisdictions, voting continued to be significantly polarized on the basis of race, with the result that blacks were unable to elect candidates of their choice even if all eligible blacks were registered, all showed up at the polls on election day, and all voted for the same candidate. Given the reality of white bloc voting, the candidates favored by black voters usually lost.

Black voters have, however, in more recent times made significant gains in officeholding. On the eve of the passage of the Voting Rights Act, there were fewer than a hundred black elected officials in the entire eleven states of the old Confederacy.[2] By January 1993, the number had grown to 4,182; by January 2000, the number stood at 5,579.[3] The key to increasing effective minority political participation and black officeholding has been the creation of majority-minority districts. Indeed, it is only the creation of these districts under the Voting Rights Act that has succeeded in blunting the effects of systematic white bloc voting. Prior to 1996, the only black in the twentieth century to win a seat in Congress from a majority-white district in the deep South states of Virginia, North Carolina, South Carolina, Georgia, Florida, Alabama, Mississippi, Louisiana, and Texas was Andrew Young. He was elected in 1972 from the Fifth District in metropolitan Atlanta, in which blacks were 44 percent of the population.[4]

A similar pattern of minority officeholding prevailed in southern state legislatures. Throughout the 1970s and 1980s, only about 1 percent of majority-white districts elected a black member. Blacks who were elected were overwhelmingly from majority-black districts.[5] As late as 1988, no black candidate had been elected from majority-white districts in Alabama, Arkansas, Louisiana, Mississippi, or South Carolina.[6] The number of blacks elected to state legislatures increased after the 1990 redistricting, but again the gain resulted from an increase in the number of majority-black districts.[7] A comprehensive and systematic study of the impact of the Voting Rights Act from 1965 to 1990, *Quiet Revolution in the South*, concluded that "the increase in the number of black elected officials is a product of the increase in the number of majority-black districts and not of blacks winning in majority-white districts."[8]

The Prevailing Legal Standards

The increase in majority-black districts in the South was driven by a number of factors, but among the most important were:

(1) The amendment of Section 2 of the Voting Rights Act in 1982 to incorporate a discriminatory "results" test; [9]
(2) The 1986 decision of the Supreme Court in *Thornburg v. Gingles*,[10] which greatly simplified the test for proving minority vote dilution;
(3) Effective enforcement by the Justice Department of Section 5 of the Voting Rights Act,[11] which requires jurisdictions with the worst histories of discrimination in voting to preclear, or get federal approval of, any changes in their election laws or practices; and
(4) A massive litigation campaign by the civil rights community.

In response to the decision of the U.S. Supreme Court in *City of Mobile v. Bolden*,[12] Congress amended Section 2 to make it clear that a voting practice, such as a districting plan, could violate the statute if it resulted in discrimination, regardless of the reasons why it was enacted or was being maintained. A discriminatory result could be shown by a variety of factors, known as "the totality of circumstances," including a history of discrimination, the existence of polarized voting, a dearth of minority elected officials, cultural and language barriers, overt or subtle racial campaign appeals, a depressed socioeconomic status, and the use of a majority vote requirement.[13] A plaintiff's ultimate burden was to show that a challenged practice diluted minority voting strength by providing minorities less opportunity than other voters to elect candidates of their choice.

Thornburg v. Gingles, the first decision of the Supreme Court regarding the amended Section 2, streamlined the test for proving a Section 2 violation. The Court identified three primary factors for deciding when a state was obligated to draw a majority-minority district:

(1) Whether the minority was sufficiently large and geographically compact enough to constitute a majority in one or more single-member districts;
(2) Whether the minority was politically cohesive, or voted as a bloc; and
(3) Whether the majority usually voted as a bloc to defeat the candidates favored by the minority.[14]

The test for vote dilution was still based on the totality of circumstances, but as the Supreme Court has held, "lack of equal electoral opportunity may be readily imagined and unsurprising when demonstrated under circumstances that include the three essential *Gingles* factors." [15]

Gingles brought both simplicity and a measure of predictability to vote dilution challenges. By placing primary emphasis on demographic data to determine compactness and election returns to determine racial bloc voting, the Court put vote dilution challenges on an evidentiary basis similar to one-person, one-vote cases and responded to the criticism that the totality of circumstances test was amorphous and lacked a definable core.

During the 1980s and 1990s, 15 new majority-black congressional districts were created in the South as a result of litigation, or threats of litigation, under Section 2 or as a result of the Section 5 preclearance process. (See Table 2.1.) Voting rights litigation in the 1980s produced majority-black districts in Georgia (the Fifth), Louisiana (the Second), and Mississippi (the Second).[16] Similar litigation in the 1990s produced a majority-black congressional district

Table 2.1
Majority-Black Congressional Districts Created in the South in Response to Litigation, Threats of Litigation, and Preclearance Objections: 1980s and 1990s

States	No. of Added Districts	Names of Districts	Total No. of New Districts
Alabama	1	7th	1
Florida	3	3rd, 17th, 23rd	3
Georgia	3	2nd, 5th, 11th	3
Louisiana	2	2nd, 4th	2
Mississippi	1	2nd	1
North Carolina	2	1st, 12th	2
South Carolina	1	6th	1
Texas	1	30th	2
Virginia	1	3rd	1

Note: Florida-23 is included because it is "near" majority black and is represented by Alcee Hastings. Other districts are majority black.

in Alabama (the Seventh), one in South Carolina (the Sixth), two in Florida (the Third and the Seventeenth), and a third district in Florida (the Twenty-third) in which blacks were 46 percent of the population and when combined with Hispanics were the majority.[17] During the 1990s, Section 5 objections or threatened objections by the attorney general also resulted in the creation of two additional majority-black districts in Georgia (the Second and the Eleventh), one additional district in Louisiana (the Fourth), and two in North Carolina (the First and the Twelfth).[18] The threat of litigation or objections to preclearance by civil rights organizations was a factor in the creation of a second majority-black district in Texas (the Thirtieth) and one in Virginia (the Third) during the 1990s.[19] The two other majority-minority districts in the South were the Ninth in Memphis and the Eighteenth in Texas.[20]

The increase in majority-black districts was followed by an increase in black elected officials. Seventeen of the majority-minority congressional districts in the South—and none of the majority-white districts—elected a black in the 1992 elections.[21] There were also substantial increases in the number of majority-minority state legislative districts and a corresponding increase in black legislators following the 1990 redistricting. In the South, the number of black state senators rose from 43 to 67, and the number of black state house members increased from 159 to 213.[22]

It is not a great exaggeration to say that during the 1980s and early 1990s, it was generally understood that if a jurisdiction could draw a majority-minority district, it had to do so. And if it did not, its plan would be denied preclearance under Section 5. And even if the plan were precleared, a court would likely set it aside under Section 2. While the U.S. Department of Justice played a critical role in the administration of Section 5, the burden of enforcing the Voting Rights Act through litigation was borne principally by the minority and civil rights communities. For the ten-year period from 1978 to 1988, the United States was a plaintiff in only 105 (5 percent) of the 2,052 voting cases filed in federal court. The rest were brought by private plaintiffs.[23]

The White Backlash

Social scientists and the courts have frequently commented on the "tipping phenomenon," a form of racial backlash that occurs when whites perceive that there has been "too much" integration and flee a neighborhood or take their children out of the public schools.[24] The 1992 elections were undoubtedly a tipping event for many whites who believed that their districts had become too black. The disaffected whites did not move or stop going to the polls, but instead asked the courts to redraw the districts so that whites would again be in the majority with the ability to exercise their traditional privilege of electing members of Congress.

The first of the backlash suits decided by the Supreme Court was *Shaw v. Reno*,[25] a challenge to congressional redistricting in North Carolina. The Court held that white voters who lived in a majority-black district had standing to challenge the district as a violation of the Equal Protection Clause of the Fourteenth Amendment based upon the district's "bizarre" shape. Two years later in *Miller v. Johnson*,[26] a challenge to congressional redistricting in Georgia, the Court enlarged the scope of *Shaw v. Reno*. It held that white voters who lived in a majority-black district could challenge the district on constitutional grounds, regardless of its shape, if race had been the "predominant" factor in drawing the district's lines.

In the wake of *Shaw* and *Miller*, the courts were flooded with challenges by white voters who claimed that the majority-black districts in which they resided were unconstitutional racial gerrymanders. Aside from the litigation in North Carolina and Georgia, lawsuits challenging congressional plans were filed in Texas, Louisiana, Florida, New York, Virginia, Illinois, South Carolina, and

Alabama.[27] Similar challenges were filed against majority-black state legislative districts in South Carolina, Florida, Texas, Georgia, Louisiana, North Carolina, and Ohio.[28] Although some commentators predicted that the new Shaw jurisprudence would be an "exceptional doctrine for aberrational contexts,"[29] one court surmised that it cast "substantial doubt as to whether legislative division into race-based districts or election areas can ever withstand constitutional scrutiny."[30] In any event, the *Shaw/Miller* jurisprudence was viewed with alarm in the civil rights community because it challenged the very mechanism—majority-minority districts—that had best advanced the promise of equal political participation held out by the Voting Rights Act.

Applying the rules in *Shaw* and *Miller*, the Supreme Court struck down majority-black districts in North Carolina, Georgia, and Texas,[31] while lower courts did the same to majority-black congressional districts in Florida, Virginia, Louisiana, and New York.[32] *Shaw/Miller* were also used to invalidate districts for state and county offices.[33]

Not all the *Shaw/Miller* challenges have succeeded. The Court summarily affirmed without opinion lower court decisions rejecting challenges to congressional plans in California and in Illinois,[34] as well as a legislative plan in Ohio.[35] The Court also affirmed the decision of the district court rejecting a challenge to legislative redistricting in Florida.[36]

The Court in the *Shaw* and *Miller* cases criticized majority-minority districts as being an "inherently suspect" form of affirmative action for minorities,[37] but the decisions were in fact a new and powerful form of affirmative action for white voters. The Court created a new cause of action where there had been none before, allowing white voters to challenge a majority-black district based solely on its shape.[38] It liberalized the doctrine of standing by dispensing with the requirement that white voters show a personal, concrete injury. Their injury, according to the Court, was in being "stereotyped" or "stigmatized" by a racial classification.[39] In prior cases involving black plaintiffs, however, the Court had held that a similar abstract, hypothetical, or stigmatic injury was not sufficient to confer standing to challenge discriminatory governmental action.[40]

Shaw also relaxed the requirement that white plaintiffs prove the state intended to discriminate against them in enacting a challenged redistricting plan. The Court reasoned that even though a districting plan appeared to be neutral, a racial classification was apparent or "express" where a majority-black district had a "bizarre" shape, and that accordingly "[n]o inquiry into legislative purpose is necessary."[41] That is different from the standard applied by the Court in voting cases brought by blacks. In *City of Mobile v. Bolden*,[42] in setting aside a constitutional challenge by black voters to municipal at-large elections, the Court stressed that "only if there is purposeful discrimination can there be a violation of the Equal Protection Clause." Even proof that black voting strength in the city had been diluted by the challenged practice was, according to the Court, "most assuredly insufficient to prove an unconstitutionally discriminatory purpose."[43]

Shaw/Miller also embodies a dual standard, depending on whether a district is majority-minority or majority-white. In the challenge to congressional redistricting in Texas, the plaintiffs challenged 24 of the state's 30 congressional districts, 18 of which were majority white.[44] The district court invalidated only three districts, the two that were majority black (the Eighteenth and the Thirtieth) and one that was majority Hispanic (the Twenty-Ninth).[45] The court admitted that the other districts were irregular or bizarre in shape, but held that they were constitutional because they were "disfigured less to favor or disadvantage one race or ethnic group than to promote the re-election of incumbents."[46] Thus, the oddly shaped majority-white districts, designed to keep white incumbents in office, were tolerable as "political" gerrymanders, while the oddly shaped majority-black districts, designed to provide black voters the equal opportunity to elect candidates of their choice, were intolerable as "racial" gerrymanders. On appeal, the Supreme Court affirmed. According to Justice Kennedy, "[d]istricts not drawn for impermissible reasons or according to impermissible criteria may take any shape, even a bizarre one."[47] The Court said in *Shaw* that "reapportionment is one area in which appearances do matter."[48] In light of the Texas case one can conclude that appearances do indeed matter, but only when the districts are majority black or Hispanic.

The new cause of action based on bizarre district shape, the special rule on standing, the absence of a requirement to show a discriminatory purpose, and the dual standard for majority-white and nonwhite districts have transformed the Fourteenth Amendment from a law designed to prohibit discrimination against racial minorities,[49] to one that can now be used to challenge majority-minority districts and allow whites to maximize their control of the electoral process.

Shaw/Miller also created substantial confusion over the extent to which the consideration of race in redistricting was prohibited by the constitution, and the extent to which it was required to avoid retrogression under Section 5 and liability under Section 2. According to the Court, a legislature may properly "be aware of racial demographics," but it may not allow race to predominate in the redistricting process.[50] A state "is free to recognize communities that have a particular racial makeup, provided its action is directed toward some common thread of relevant interests."[51] Redistricting may be performed "with consciousness of race."[52] Indeed, it would be "irresponsible" for a state to disregard the racial fairness provisions of the Voting Rights Act.[53] A state may therefore "create a majority minority district without awaiting judicial findings" if it has a strong basis in evidence for avoiding a Voting Rights Act violation.[54] The Court majority has acknowledged that it "may be difficult" to make and apply such distinctions.[55]

The justices who dissented in the *Shaw* cases have charged that the Court's standards are "unworkable,"[56] lack "a definable constitutional core,"[57] "render redistricting perilous work for state legislatures,"[58] and "place at a disadvantage the very group, African Americans, whom the Civil War Amendments sought to help."[59] They are also a prescription for litigation. A jurisdiction is subject to a Voting Rights Act challenge if it fails to create majority-minority districts to remedy vote dilution but it is subject to a Fourteenth Amendment challenge if it does.

Assessing the Impact of *Shaw/Miller*

Shaw/Miller has had an undeniable impact, but the worst predictions that it would systematically roll back the gains in minority office holding have not come to pass. That they have not is attributable to the advantages of incumbency, the continuing vitality of the Voting Rights Act, the increased influence of black elected officials, and the willingness of white Democrats, in the face of the rise of the Republican party, to support the reelection of their black Democratic colleagues.

The incumbent blacks who were drawn into majority-white congressional districts as a result of *Shaw/Miller* litigation were all re-elected except Cleo Fields of Louisiana, who declined to run. In contrast, all non-incumbent blacks who ran in majority-white congressional districts in the South in 1996 (Arkansas, Mississippi, and Texas) lost.[60] Cynthia McKinney, one of the incumbents who was re-elected, has credited her victory to the fact that she was initially elected in a majority-black district (the old Eleventh) and thus had an opportunity to establish a track record of service to constituents of both races and to ameliorate white fears over being represented by a black.[61] The power of incumbency is substantial and has been described as the single best indicator of electoral outcome.[62] Nationwide, more than 90 percent of incumbent house members who sought reelection in 1996 won, including all 11 incumbents from Georgia.[63]

Despite *Shaw/Miller*, covered jurisdictions still have to comply with Section 5, and where they have enacted retrogressive plans, they have drawn objections from the Justice Department or the District Court for the District of Columbia. In 1997, the attorney general objected to senate redistricting in South Carolina, which had been undertaken in response to a court decision invalidating three of the state's senate districts on *Shaw/Miller* grounds. In objecting to the reconfiguration of District 37, the attorney general concluded that "the significant reduction in black voting strength" was unnecessary for the state to comply with the federal court orders.[64] More recently, the attorney general has objected to legislative redistricting in Texas, Arizona, and Florida on the grounds that minority voting strength was unnecessarily reduced in various districts in the state.[65] At the local level, the attorney general continued to object to redistricting and other voting practices upon concluding that they caused retrogression in minority voting strength.[66]

When federal courts have been called upon to implement interim court-ordered plans following a state's failure to redistrict in a timely manner, they have also applied both the non-retrogression standard of Section 5 and the racial fairness standard of Section 2. The three-judge court in *Colleton County Council v. McConnell*[67] (a case that was filed after the governor and the legislature in South Carolina deadlocked over redistricting in 2001) acknowledged the constraints placed on it by *Shaw/Miller*. However, the court concluded that it was also obligated to comply with Sections 2 and 5 of the Voting Rights Act and proceeded to draw plans that maintained the existing majority-black congressional district and actually increased the number of majority-black house and senate districts.[68] In Mississippi, which lost a congressional seat as a result of the 2000 Census, both the state and the federal courts became involved in the redistricting process. Relying upon the nonretrogression standard of Section 5, the courts drew plans that maintained one of the districts as majority black.[69]

The Myth of the Colorblind Political Process

The redistricting that has taken place since *Shaw/Miller* shows conclusively, if such proof were needed, that the political process is not in fact colorblind, and that taking race into account is a political reality. Both major political parties are acutely aware of the importance of the minority vote, and in the redistricting that has followed the 2000 Census both have done their best to manipulate it to their own partisan advantage. Democrats have typically drawn plans reducing black majorities in existing districts to the minimum necessary to provide a bare 50-50 chance of electing a candidate of choice, so that the remaining black voters could be spread to neighboring districts to provide opportunities for the election of white Democrats.

In an unsuccessful attempt to preclear its 2001 senate redistricting plan, the State of Georgia, under Democratic control, argued before a three-judge court in the District of Columbia that reducing the black voting age population from a majority to 44.3 percent was not retrogressive because the redrawn districts provided black voters an "equal opportunity," or a 50-50 chance, to elect candidates of their choice.[70] White voters, not to mention white incumbents, would hardly be content with districts that provided them with a 50-50 chance of winning or losing. More important, the Voting Rights Act guarantees minorities an equal, not a bare 50-50, opportunity to elect candidates of their choice. In rejecting the state's plan, the three-judge court held that the purpose of Section 5 was to determine whether a proposed change would "decrease" minority voters' electoral opportunities, and that the reductions in black population in the districts at issue "may have a significant...negative impact on the likelihood that African American voters will be able to elect their candidates of choice."[71]

Republicans, on the other hand, typically have tried to pack existing majority-black districts with black voters to increase the likelihood that the neighboring "bleached" districts will elect white Republicans. And they have done so under the guise of enforcing Sections 2 and 5 of the Voting Rights Act. Minority voters, caught in the middle of this partisan struggle, are at risk of being either "packed" by Republicans or "cracked" by Democrats.

In *Colleton County Council*, the three-judge court took special note that the governor and the legislature "have proposed plans that are primarily driven by policy choices designed to effect their particular partisan goals."[72] Those choices included protecting incumbents and assigning the minority population to maximize the parties' respective political opportunities. As explained by the court:

> By increasing the BVAP [black voting age population] percentage in Republican-held districts, the Governor increases the probability of a white Democrat ousting the Republican incumbent in the general election but at the expense of lowering the BVAP in an adjoining majority minority district and the concomitant ability for blacks to elect a black Democrat in that district over a white Democrat. By increasing the BVAP in current majority minority districts, the Senate Republicans avoid that result and make the adjoining 'super-white' districts Republican strongholds.[73]

Minority officeholders, who are predominantly Democratic, have frequently supported their party's efforts to reduce black majorities to create opportunities for white Democrats. They have done so on the premise that as incumbents they can survive the reductions in their black populations and that the election of white Democrats ultimately benefits the black community. Congressman John Lewis in his testimony in the Georgia case made no apologies for supporting plans that would maximize Democratic control of the state legislature. "[I]f black elected officials, black state legislators, are going to have any sense of control, any sense of power, as chairs of full committees or chairs of subcommittees, it will come with being in the majority," he said. "So, it's in our best interest for us to maintain a Democratic-controlled state legislature. I think that's important. I think this is a must."[74]

Only two members of the Georgia black caucus voted against the state's senate redistricting plan. The votes in favor of the plan, which were essential to its passage, underscore the extent to which minorities have been included in the decisionmaking process by the Democratic party, which views such inclusion as central to the party's survival in the face of the growth of the Republican party in the state. The district court, however, rejected the state's senate plan under Section 5 because it diluted minority voting strength in three urban areas of the state—Albany, Macon, and Savannah.[75] The court concluded that while the support of the plan by black legislators was relevant to the issue of discriminatory purpose, it was "dubious evidence" of a plan's possible retrogressive effect. "A vote for legislation," the court reasoned, "is almost always a compromise of some sort, motivated by a complex intersection of self-interest and external pressure."[76] In any event, the essential purpose of the Voting Rights Act is to protect the rights of minority voters. The fact that a plan protects minority incumbents, or promotes the interests of a minority friendly political party, cannot immunize the plan from retrogression of minority voting strength under Section 5.[77]

A Green Light to Partisan Gerrymandering

Partisan gerrymandering, at least when performed by a legislature, was given a boost in *Easley v. Cromartie.*[78] The Supreme Court in *Easley* rejected an equal protection challenge to congressional redistricting in North Carolina, concluding that politics, not race, was the predominant factor in drawing the state's plan. While the legislature had plainly considered race, the Court concluded that the plaintiffs had failed to carry their burden of proof that race "predominated" in the drawing of district lines.[79] Neither the majority opinion nor the dissent so much as mentioned *Davis v. Bandemer*, in which the Court held that partisan gerrymandering could rise to the level of a constitutional violation "when the electoral system is arranged in a manner that will consistently degrade a voter's or a group of voters' influence on the political process as a whole."[80]

Easley was widely seen as providing a way of avoiding *Shaw/Miller* challenges in drawing majority-black or near majority-black districts (politics, not race, made us do it), and giving the green light for aggressive partisan gerrymandering. Some of the majority-white districts drawn in the aftermath of *Easley*—for example, state senate Districts 16 and 24 in Georgia drawn by the Democratic-controlled legislature—are utterly bizarre in shape and would doubtlessly never withstand a *Shaw/Miller* challenge were they majority black. Whether these districts survive the challenges that may be mounted against them on state law and other grounds by the political party injured by the partisan gerrymandering, remains to be seen. But one factor, absent a sea change in the law, will remain constant. Only the attempts of racial minorities to draw districts that provide them with equal electoral opportunities will be subject to strict constitutional scrutiny. Such a result is surely inconsistent with the original, and true, meaning of the Fourteenth Amendment. As Justice Stevens wrote in his dissenting opinion in *Shaw*:

> If it is permissible to draw boundaries to provide adequate representation for rural voters, for union members, for Hasidic Jews, for Polish Americans, or for Republicans, it necessarily follows that it is permissible to do the same thing for members of the very minority group whose history in the United States gave birth to the Equal Protection Clause.[81]

NOTES

1 *Harper v. Virginia State Board of Elections*, 383 U.S. 663 (1966).

2 U.S. Commission on Civil Rights, *Political Participation* (Washington, D.C.: U.S. Government Printing Office, 1968), 15.

3 Joint Center for Political and Economic Studies, *Black Elected Officials: A National Roster* (Lanham, MD: University Press of America, 1993), xxiii. This is not to suggest that blacks were elected to office in proportion to their presence in the population. While blacks were 19.2 percent of the region's population based on the 1990 Census, they were only 6.1 percent of its elected officials. Id. at 1, 39, 93, 105, 175, 237, 319, 377, 399, 409, 439.

4 Michael Barone and Grant Ujifusa, *The Almanac of American Politics* (Boston: Gambit, 1974), 232.

5 Lisa Handley and Bernard Grofman, "The Impact of the Voting Rights Act on Minority Representation: Black Officeholding in Southern State Legislatures and Congressional Delegations," in *Quiet Revolution in the South*, edited by C. Davidson and B. Grofman (Princeton, NJ: Princeton University Press, 1994), 336-337.

6 Id. at 346.

7 David A. Bositis, *Redistricting and Representation: The Creation of Majority-Minority Districts and the Evolving Party System in the South* (Washington, DC: Joint Center for Political and Economic Studies, 1995), 46.

8 Handle and Grofman, "The Impact of the Voting Rights Act on Minority Representation," 335.

9 42 U.S.C. § 1973.

10 478 U.S. 30 (1986).

11 42 U.S.C. § 1973c.

12 446 U.S. 55 (1980).

13 S.Rep. No. 417, 97th Cong., 2d Sess. 28-9 (1982).

14 478 U.S. at 50-1.

15 *Johnson v. De Grandy*, 512 U.S. 997, 1012 (1994).

16 *Busbee* v. *Smith*, 549 F. Supp. 494 (D.D.C. 1982); *Major v. Treen*, 574 F. Supp. 325, 355 (E.D.La. 1983); *Jordan v. Winter*, 604 F. Supp. 807, 813 (N.D. Miss. 1984).

17 *Wesch v. Hunt*, 785 F. Supp. 1491, 1498-99 (S.D. Ala. 1992); *Burton v. Sheheen*, 793 F. Supp. 1329, 1367-1369 (D.S.C. 1992); *DeGrandy v. Wetherell*, 794 F. Supp. 1076, 1088 (N.D. Fla. 1992).

18 *Johnson v. Miller*, 864 F. Supp. 1354, 1366 (S.D.Ga. 1994); *Hays v. Louisiana*, 839 F. Supp. 1188, 1196 n.21 (W.D. La. 1993); *Shaw v. Barr*, 808 F. Supp. 461, 464 (E.D.N.C.1992).

19 *Vera v. Richards*, 861 F. Supp. 1304, 1315 (S.D.Tex. 1994) (noting the testimony before a senate committee of a director of Texas Rural Legal Aid that unless an additional black congressional district were created "the reapportionment of the Congress is not going to pass the Department of Justice"); Bill Wasson, "Wilder Plan Expected to Win Assembly OK," *The Richmond News Leader*, Dec. 3, 1991, at 1 (ACLU and NAACP prepared to

challenge state plan if Governor "didn't increase black voting strength in the 3rd District").

20 Barone and Ujifusa, *The Almanac of American Politics.*

21 "1990 U.S. Census, Population and Housing Profile, Congressional Districts of the 103rd Congress," *C.Q. Weekly Report* 51, 3473-3487.

22 Bositis, *Redistricting and Representation,* 46-47.

23 Annual Reports of the Director of the Administrative Office of the United States Courts, Table C 2, U.S. District Courts, Civil Cases Commenced, by Basis of Jurisdiction and Nature of Suit, June 30, 1978-June 30, 1988.

24 See, e.g., A. Leon Higginbotham, Jr., et al., "*Shaw v. Reno*: A Mirage of Good Intentions with Devastating Racial Consequences," 62 *Fordham Law Review* 1593, 1632 n.194 (1994); Richard H. Pildes, "The Politics of Race," 108 *Harvard Law Review* 1359, 1382 (1995) ("[a]s the Black population reaches a critical mass, White voters begin to see Black participation as a credible threat; in reaction, White voters band together and develop more conservative preferences").

25 509 U.S. 630 (1993).

26 515 U.S. 900 (1995).

27 *Vera* v. *Richards,* 861 F. Supp. at 1309; *Hays v. Louisiana,* 839 F. Supp. at 1190-91; *Johnson* v. *Mortham,* 926 F. Supp. 1460 (N.D.Fla. 1996); *Diaz* v. *Silver,* 932 F. Supp. 462 (E.D.N.Y. 1996); *Moon* v. *Meadows,* 952 F. Supp. 1141 (E.D.Va. 1997); *King* v. *State Board of Elections,* 979 F. Supp. 582 (N.D.Ill. 1996); *Leonard* v. *Beasley,* Civ. No. 3:96-CV-3540 (D.S.C.); *McKee v. James,* No. CV-97-C-2078-W (N.D.ALA.).

28 *Smith v. Beasly,* 946 F. Supp. 1174, 1175 (D.S.C. 1996); *Scott v. U.S. Dept. of Justice,* 920 F. Supp. 1248 (M.D.Fla. 1996); *Thomas v. Bush,* No. A-95-CA 18655 (W.D.Tex.); *Johnson v. Miller,* 929 F. Supp. 1529 (S.D.Ga. 1996); *Currie v. Foster,* No. 97-CV-368 (W.D.La.); *Daly v. High,* No. 5:96 CV 86-V (W.D.N.C.); *Quilter v. Voinovich,* 912 F. Supp. 1006 (N.D.Oh. 1995).

29 Richard H. Pildes and Richard G. Niemi, "Expressive Harms, 'Bizarre Districts,' and Voting Rights: Evaluating Election-District Appearances After *Shaw v. Reno,*" 92 *Mich. L. Rev.* 483, 495 (1993).

30 *Lopez v. Monterey County,* No. C-91-20559-RMW, slip op. at 3 (N.D.Cal. Nov. 1, 1995).

31 *Shaw v. Hunt,* 517 U.S. 899 (1996) (District Twelve in North Carolina); *Miller v. Johnson,* 515 U.S. at 928 (District Eleven in Georgia); *Abrams* v. *Johnson,* 521 U.S. 74 (1997) (District Two in Georgia); *Bush v. Vera,* 517 U.S. 952 (1996) (Districts Eighteen, Twenty-Nine, and Thirty in Texas).

32 *Johnson v. Mortham,* 926 F. Supp. at 1495 (District Three in Florida); *Moon v. Meadows,* 952 F. Supp. at 1150 (District Three in Virginia); *Hays v. Louisiana,* 936 F. Supp. 360, 371 (W.D.La. 1996) (District Four in Louisiana); *Diaz v. Silver,* 978 F. Supp. 96 (E.D.N.Y. 1997) (District Twelve in New York).

33 See, e.g., *Johnson v. Miller,* 929 F. Supp. 1529 (S.D.Ga. 1996) (legislative districts in Georgia); *Smith v. Beasley,* 946 F. Supp. 1174 (D.S.C. 1996) (legislative districts in South Carolina); *Clark v. Putnam County,* 293 F. 3d 1261 (11th Cir. 2002) (county commission district in Georgia).

34 *DeWitt v. Wilson*, 515 U.S. 1170 (1995); *King v. Illinois Board of Election*, 522 U.S. 1087 (1998), aff'g, 979 F. Supp. 582, 619 (N.D.Ill. 1996).

35 *Quilter v. Voinovich*, 981 F. Supp. 1032 (N.D.Ohio 1997), aff'd, 523 U.S. 1043 (1998).

36 *Lawyer v. Department of Justice*, 521 U.S. 567 (1997).

37 *Miller v. Johnson*, 515 U.S. at 915, citing *Regents of University of California v. Bakke*, 438 U.S. 265, 291 (1978) (opinion of Powell, J.).

38 In *Gaffney v. Cummings*, 412 U.S. 735, 752 n.18 (1973), the Court had rejected the notion that district "compactness or attractiveness . . . [was] an independent federal constitutional requirement."

39 *Miller v. Johnson*, 515 U.S. at 912-13; *Shaw v. Reno*, 509 U.S. at 643. *Lawyer v. Department of Justice*, 521 U.S. 567 (1997).

40 *Allen v. Wright*, 468 U.S. 737, 754 (1984).

41 *Shaw v. Reno*, 509 U.S. at 642.

42 446 U.S. 55, 66 (1980).

43 Id. at 73.

44 *Vera v. Richards*, 861 F. Supp. at 1309.

45 Id. at 1343-44.

46 Id. at 1309.

47 *Bush v. Vera*, 517 U.S. at 999.

48 *Shaw v. Reno*, 509 U.S. at 647.

49 See the Slaughter-House Cases, 83 U.S. (16 Wall) 36, 81 (1873) (the Fourteenth Amendment was adopted to remedy "discrimination against the Negroes as a class, or on account of their race").

50 *Miller v. Johnson*, 515 U.S. at 916.

51 Id. at 920.

52 *Bush v. Vera*, 517 U.S. at 958.

53 Id. at 991 (O'Connor, J., concurring).

54 Id. at 994.

55 *Miller v. Johnson*, 515 U.S. at 916.

56 *Abrams v. Johnson*, 521 U.S. at 116 (Breyer, J., dissenting); *Bush v. Vera*, 517 U.S. at 1074 ("[t]he Court has been unable to provide workable standards") (Souter, J. dissenting).

57 *Bush v. Vera*, 517 U.S. at 1005 (Stevens, J., dissenting).

58 *Miller v. Johnson*, 515 U.S. at 949 (Ginsburg, J., dissenting).

59 *Abrams v. Johnson*, 521 U.S. at 118 (Breyer, J. dissenting).

60 David A. Bositis, "The Future of Majority-Minority Districts and Black and Hispanic Legislative Representation," in *Redistricting and Minority Representation*, edited by David A. Bositis (Washington, DC: Joint Center for Political and Economic Studies, 1998) 38-39. Vincent Tolliver was defeated in Arkansas' Fourth District (6% black

VAP), Kevin Antoine was defeated in Mississippi's Fourth District (37% black VAP), and Teresa Doggett was defeated in Texas' Tenth District (10% black VAP). Id.

61 Cynthia A. McKinney, "A Product of the Voting Rights Act," *Washington Post*, Nov. 26, 1996, p. A15 ("my victory says more about the power of incumbency than anything else").

62 Bositis, "The Future of Majority-Minority Districts," note 60.

63 Michael A. Fletcher, "New Tolerance in the South Or Old Power of Incumbency?" *Washington Post*, Nov. 23, 1996, p. A1; Kevin Sack, "Victory of 5 Redistricted Blacks Recasts Gerrymandering Dispute," *New York Times*, Nov. 23, 1996, p. 8.

64 Isabelle Katz Pinzler to John W. Drummond, April 1, 1997.

65 Ralph F. Boyd, Jr. to Geoffrey Conner, Nov. 16, 2001 (objecting to the reduction of minority voting strength in Bexar County, South Texas, and West Texas); Ralph F. Boyd, Jr. to Lisa T. Hauser, May 20, 2002 (objecting to the configuration of five legislative districts in Arizona); Ralph F. Boyd, Jr. to John M. McKay, July 1, 2002 (objecting to house redistricting in Collier County, Florida).

66 See, e.g., Isabel Katz Pinzler to George W. McHugh, Oct. 6, 1997(objecting to redistricting for St. Martinville, LA); Bill Lann Lee to E. Paul Jones, Feb. 6, 1998 (objecting to a redistricting plan for Tallapoosa County, Alabama).

67 201 F. Supp. 2d 618 (D.S.C. 2002).

68 The benchmark applied by the court for determining retrogression in house redistricting was 25 majority-black districts. The court-ordered plan increased that number to 29. The benchmark for senate redistricting was nine majority-black districts. The court's plan maintained the nine districts and created an additional district that contained a sufficient minority population to allow minority voters an equal opportunity to elect a candidate of their choice. 201 F. Supp. 2d at 655-56, 661, 666.

69 *Smith* v. *Clark*, 189 F. Supp. 2d 529, 535, 540 (S.D. Miss. 2002).

70 *Georgia* v. *Ashcroft*, 195 F. Supp. 2d 25, 80 (D.D.C. 2002).

71 Id. at 82.

72 201 F. Supp. 2d at 628.

73 Id. at 659.

74 *Georgia* v. *Ashcroft*, 195 F. Supp. 2d at 92.

75 Id. at 55.

76 Id. at 89.

77 Id. at 93.

78 532 U.S. 234 (2001).

79 Id. at 257.

80 478 U.S. 109, 132 (1986).

81 509 U.S. at 679.

3. Political Parties, Redistricting, and Minority Representation: The Southern States, 1992-2002

David A. Bositis

Although it has declined somewhat in recent years, racially polarized voting continues to be a defining condition of Southern politics. Race was the single most important reason for the growth of the Republican Party in the South since the civil rights era; hence, race is largely responsible for the dynamics of the current two-party system in the United States. Non-Hispanic whites predominate in all parts of the Republican Party—its elected and organization leadership, partisans in the public, and voting supporters. From President Bush to the top leaders in the U.S. Senate and House, the Republican national leadership is dominated by southerners, making the South the party's center of gravity.[1]

In contrast, the Democratic Party is multiracial, with African Americans and Hispanics in leadership positions across the country. In elections, African Americans remain overwhelmingly Democratic, with nine in ten voting Democratic. Hispanic voters also favor Democrats. According to the exit polls, Gore received 67 percent of the Hispanic vote in the 2000 election, while Bush received 31 percent-even though he mounted a major effort to woo Hispanic voters.

Voting in Presidential Elections

The 2000 Presidential vote provides one view of racially polarized voting in the South (Figure 3.1). More than 50 years ago, V.O. Key noted that the importance of race was greater in the "deep South" than in the "border South."[2] Characterized by proportionally large black populations, the states of the deep South are those that run in a band from Louisiana to South Carolina (Louisiana, Mississippi, Alabama, Georgia, South Carolina).

Not surprisingly, the 2000 Presidential vote still largely follows the pattern of racially polarized voting identified by Key. The states of the deep South had the largest gaps between black and white votes cast for Gore.[3] Mississippi had the greatest division between black and white voters—79 percentage points—with Gore receiving 96 percent of the black vote and 17 percent of the white vote. The remaining deep South states had differences that ranged between 65 and 66 percent, with Gore receiving 26 percent of the white vote and between 91 and 92 percent of the black vote. In the border South (except Texas), the gap between black and white voters was smaller, with Gore receiving between 31 and 41 percent of the white vote and between 84 and 93 percent of the black vote. The racial gap was smallest in Arkansas with 42 percentage points separating black and white voters, a gap that is only slightly more than half the division between black and white voters in Mississippi.

Black versus White Candidates in U.S. House Elections

Between 1990 and 2000, forty-eight U.S. House races in the South featured black and white opponents (Table 3.1). During this period, every southern state had at least one of these contests. Black candidates won 40 of these contests and lost eight. All black incumbents won, and the seven black non-incumbents were elected in open-seat contests in majority-minority districts. Of the eight black candidates who lost, one ran in a majority Hispanic district, and the other seven ran in districts with majority populations that were non-Hispanic white. Three of the losing black candidates were Republicans, and all but two faced opponents who were incumbents.

A regression analysis for these races suggests that the vote for the black candidates was dependent on the black voting-age population (BVAP) of the district and incumbency status.[4] The two-variable model had reasonably good explanatory power, with 75 percent of the variance in the vote for the black candidate explained by the two factors. The model equation is:[5]

$$\text{Black candidate vote} = 31.7 + 0.50 \bullet \text{BVAP} + 10.7 \bullet \text{Incumbency status}$$

The implications of this model are as follows: a black incumbent would need a BVAP of at least 15.2 percent to win (i.e., 50+ percent) against a white opponent in the South, a black candidate in an open-seat contest would need a BVAP of at least 36.6 percent to win,[6] and a black candidate facing a white incumbent opponent would require a district with a BVAP of at least 58 percent.

These implications, however, bear further scrutiny. First, to become an incumbent, a black candidate would have to run in either a majority-minority district or in an open-seat election with a BVAP of at least 36.6 percent. Therefore, a black incumbent would never run in a district with a 15.2 percent BVAP.[7] Further, at this time in the South, it is highly unlikely that a white incumbent would be elected from a district with a 58 percent BVAP, even if it were a newly drawn district. Therefore, the only interesting finding from the model is the 36.6 percent BVAP needed for a black candidate to win in an open-seat contest.

In the post-2000 redistricting, only two districts meet this criteria, Georgia—12 with 43 percent black population and Georgia—13 with 42 percent black population. In the November 2002 election, two prominent black candidates—Charles Walker, Jr., and David Scott—were the Democratic nominees in these new open-seat districts. Walker lost with 45 percent of the vote, and Scott won with 59 percent of the vote. The outcomes of the two elections obviously offer limited support for the model. During the Walker campaign, however, it was revealed that he had an arrest record and other personal indiscretions, which quite likely contributed to his defeat.

The Major Parties

As noted above, in examining black and white voting choices—especially in the South—the Democratic and Republican parties define substantial racial cleavages. According to the exit polls, in the 2000 Presidential election, black voters favored Gore over Bush, 91 to 8 percent. Nationally, non-Hispanic white voters favored Bush over Gore 54 to 42 percent. As noted above, in most southern states, and especially in the deep South, white support for Gore was much less; in Mississippi, it was only 17 percent.

These racial differences can also be viewed from the perspective of what black and Hispanic voters contribute to the Republican and Democratic vote. In 2000, black and Hispanic voters represented 6.2 percent of Bush's total vote. In contrast, black and Hispanic voters represented 28.5 percent of Gore's total vote.[8] This disparity is important because elected officials are principally attentive to and support the agenda of those groups whose votes elect them and secondarily to the interests of voters from groups that they believe could be persuaded to vote for them.

The parties are not defined by voters alone. V.O. Key introduced the tripartite definition of party: the party-in-the-electorate (voters and identifiers), the party organization, and the party in office.[9] Clearly, from the perspective of the party-in-the-electorate, the GOP is the party of non-Hispanic white voters, and the Democratic Party is the party of blacks, Hispanics, and whites.

In organizational structure, the Republican Party reflects the voters who support them. At the 2000 Republican National Convention, 4.1 percent of the delegates were African Americans; at the 2000 Democratic convention, 20.1 percent of the delegates were black. In addition, at the Republican convention, there were only six black members on the convention committees (Platform, Rules, and Credentials), while at the Democratic convention, 101 black members served on the convention committees, and the co-chair of the Platform committee was black.

More important than the conventions from an organizational perspective are the national and state party committees. At the time of the 2000 conventions, only one of 153 members on the Republican National Committee was African American.[10] At that time, there were 91 black members on the Democratic National Committee (21.1 percent). Further, in state parties across the country, African American Republicans in official positions are usually found in "outreach" positions rather than in regular party leadership positions such as chair, vice-chair, treasurer, or secretary.[11] In contrast, in state and local Democratic parties across the country, African Americans hold top leadership positions.

Black elected officials are overwhelmingly Democratic. In the U.S. House of Representatives, there are 38 black Democrats; the one black Republican in the U.S. House, J.C. Watts (OK) did not seek re-election. Since most black elected officials are elected to nonpartisan offices, the best way to determine partisan affiliation among black elected officials is to look at the partisan status of state legislators. Of 592 black state legislators, only three are Republicans (two state representatives and one state senator). The three black Republicans are from Nevada, New Jersey, and Oregon; none is from the South.[12]

Black representation is intimately linked to the current party system. Since most African Americans do not view the Republican Party as a viable alternative in elections, they must seek representation in a one-party system.[13] White voters seek representation in a two-party system. This fact has important implications for redistricting, racially polarized voting, and representation — especially in the South where most African Americans live. During the 1992-2002 redistricting cycle, the redistricting process in many states was characterized by manipulation of black populations by both Republicans and Democrats for partisan advantage. Republicans sought to "pack" black voters into a small number of majority-black districts, and Democrats sought to reduce the black population in majority-minority districts in order to provide voting support for white Democratic candidates in neighboring districts.

Heterogeneous Districts, Racially Polarized Voting, and Party Primaries

In the 2000 redistricting cycle, most of the members of the Congressional Black Caucus (CBC) made a conscious decision to support Democratic Party efforts to shift black voters from majority-black districts in order to benefit party nominees (usually white) in neighboring districts. Since the membership of the CBC is entirely Democratic—and since the Democrats are in the minority in the U.S. House—CBC member influence would greatly increase if the Democrats were to regain the majority. For this reason, the CBC was willing to agree to move reliably Democratic black voters to nearby white majority districts where white Democrats would have better prospects of winning.

In many instances, African American voters in these new "black" districts were either a scant majority or merely represented a plurality of voters in the districts after blocs of black voters were moved to other districts. Prior to 2002, this strategy seemed reasonable to many voting rights advocates and black political activists because of the desirability of helping the Democrats regain majority status—and because in most of these cases incumbency afforded CBC members a high degree of security in their re-election campaigns. However, in August 2002, in the Democratic primary in Georgia, CBC member Cynthia McKinney was defeated (with 42 percent of the vote) in an election characterized by extreme racially polarized voting and reports of organized Republican crossover voting.[14]

Rep. McKinney's opponent in the primary, Rep. Denise Majette, also is an African American. Many observers—especially in the media—tend to downplay or dismiss the idea of racially polarized voting when both candidates are black. However, the Voting Rights Act addresses the issue of the rights of minority voters, and racially polarized voting, not the issue of the rights of minority candidates.[15]

U.S. House District 4 in Georgia was drawn in 2002 with a black voting-age population of 50.02 percent and an Hispanic voting-age population of 8.47

percent. In the August 2002 Georgia Democratic primary, black turnout was 30 percent and white turnout was 39 percent. On primary election day, white voters outnumbered black voters by 53.4 to 46.6 percent of all votes cast. The scatterplots of the votes for McKinney and Majette by racial composition of the precincts clearly show the impact of race on the votes for the two candidates. (See Figures 3.2 and 3.3)

Regression analyses were performed using precinct-level data to assess the impact of race on the vote in the election. The model equation for Rep. McKinney's vote was:

McKinney vote = 0.053 + 0.795 • Black voting-age population.

The model equation explains 98.7 percent of the variation in the McKinney vote; needless to say, the relationship is statistically significant (F = 16.7 with 1 degree of freedom). A one-variable linear model rarely explains this amount of variation, which suggests the extreme degree of racially polarized voting in this contest. The model suggests that McKinney received 5.4 percent of the vote in precincts with no black voters. Further, the model suggests that McKinney received 84.9 percent of the vote in precincts that were 100 percent black.

Majette's support was based among white voters. The model equation for her support was:

Majette vote = 0.161 + 0.804 • White voting-age population.

The model suggests that Majette would receive 16.1 percent of the vote in an all-black precinct, and 96.5 percent in an all-white precinct. The outcome of the election and the racial polarization in the vote were clear: McKinney received 84.9 percent of the black vote, and Majette received 96.5 percent of the white vote.

The outcome of the Democratic primary in Georgia-4 in 2002 has some significant implications for voting rights and drawing majority-minority districts. First, the new district drawn after the 2000 census clearly failed to ensure that black voters could elect their preferred candidate. The second and perhaps more important long-term impact of the McKinney-Majette election, may be to make black activists, black organizations, and black Democrats less receptive to the idea of moving black voters to white Democratic districts. This reluctance was the norm during the post-1990 redistricting, but was replaced by a more pro-Democratic posture during the 2000 redistricting.

Racial Apartheid

Two persistent, though generally misunderstood, issues in redistricting are allegations of political apartheid and balkanization. Critics of majority-minority districts have frequently employed those terms in stating their opposition to creation of these districts. Quite frankly, a sober appreciation of the facts regarding majority-minority districts can do nothing other than demonstrate that while these claims may be rhetorically seductive, they are nonetheless false.

The most racially and ethnically diverse congressional districts in the South are the majority-minority districts; this was true both before and after reapportionment in the early 1990s (Figures 3.4a and 3.4b), and it remains true in the 2000 redistricting (Figures 3.5a and 3.5b).[16] In the new redistricting, nonminority districts are the most racially homogeneous in the South, even though they are considerably more heterogeneous than in the post-1990 redistricting.

Prior to the 2000 reapportionment, the average nonminority district in the South had a variation ratio of 26 percent, that is, 74 percent of the average district's voters were in the modal (white) category. The average Hispanic district scored 29 percent diverse, meaning 71 percent of the district's voters were Hispanic. The average majority-black district scored 44 percent diverse, meaning 56 percent of the district's voters were African Americans. The average across the South's 125 districts before the 2000 reapportionment was 28 percent.

Following reapportionment, the average nonminority district in the South had a variation ratio of 25.3 percent, meaning that 74.7 percent of the district's voters were non-Hispanic whites. The average Hispanic district was more diverse than before at 35 percent, that is, 65 percent of the district's voting-age population was Hispanic. The average black district was more diverse than any others and more diverse than before at 47 percent, or 53 percent African American. The average across the South's 131 districts after reapportionment was 28.4 percent, essentially unchanged from the 2000 count for the old districts, but a huge increase (29 percent) from the original districts of the 103rd Congress (elected in 1992).

In sum, all U.S. House districts are more diverse following the 2000 redistricting, and black districts are the most diverse. Contrary to the "balkanization" hypothesis, U.S. House districts in the South—especially minority districts—are quite heterogenous in their voting populations.

Black voters are not segregated in black majority districts (Figure 3.6). First, as noted above, black districts in the South are very heterogenous, averaging 47 percent non-black populations. In 2000, the proportion of the U.S. black voting-age population residing in districts represented by Congressional Black Caucus (CBC) members was 35.8 percent. In the post-1980 redistricting, 24.8 percent of the country's black voting-age population lived in CBC districts. After the post-1990 redistricting, 42.4 percent of the nation's black voting-age population lived in those districts—an all-time high. The U.S. Supreme Court's 1993 decision in *Shaw* v. *Reno* (which was elaborated on in *Miller* v. *Johnson*) concluded that race could not be the predominant factor in constructing majority-minority districts. Since then, the number of these districts was reduced, and by the end of the decade, the share of the black voting-age population in districts represented by CBC members was little more than a third. Thus, those arguing the "apartheid" and "balkanization" hypotheses are discussing districts that individually are the most heterogeneous and collectively represent slightly more than a third of the black voting-age population in the country.

Southern State Legislatures

Two final issues that relate to representation need to be addressed: first, the impact of majority-minority districts in changing the partisan balance in southern states and in the U.S. House of Representatives, and second, whether such districts are necessary to give minority voters a chance to elect their preferred candidates.

Whether the creation of minority districts led to the ascendancy of the Republican Party in the South and in the U.S. House remains an issue of considerable debate. The facts are clear: Republicans achieved a majority in the U.S. House shortly after the 1990 redistricting, largely due to gains in the South. And, since the preponderance of black federal and state legislators are Democrats, a shift to Republican control represents a diminution of their power, and hence, diminished black representation in the legislatures. Clearly, this is what happened with the CBC starting in 1995. In the southern state legislatures prior to the 1990s redistricting, all but one black southern state legislator served with the majority in their respective chambers. By 1994, 16.1 percent of black southern state legislators served in the minority (Table 3.2). At the present time, 21.9 percent of black southern state legislators serve in the minority.[17] Of course, the number of black southern legislators has increased from 202 prior to the 1990 redistricting to 288 at present. The number of black southern legislators serving in the majority has also increased—from 201 to 225.

In the South, black majority districts are still needed to achieve black representation (Table 3.3). All but a handful of the 288 black state legislators currently serving in the South represent majority-black districts. Thus, until racially polarized voting diminishes further in the South, majority-minority districts will be necessary. The tremendous growth in the number of these districts that followed the 1990 census, however, will not continue. In the post-2000 period, we are unlikely to repeat the more-than-40 percent growth (post-1990) in black state legislators that occurred post-1990. But the new southern state legislative districts do offer some favorable prospects for black representation. First, the number of new black-majority districts is larger than the number of current southern black legislators by five (one House district and four Senate districts). However, the new redistricting also includes 19 House districts and seven Senate districts in which African Americans represent a plurality. Assuming that black candidates could be elected in those districts—and many black candidates have been elected in such districts, especially when there is a sizable Hispanic population—the potential for growth in the number of black southern state legislators in this redistricting cycle would be approximately 10 percent.

Some Concluding Thoughts

On balance, the position of black voters, voting rights activists, and black political leaders is much more precarious in the post-2002 period than in the early 1990s. Racially polarized voting remains a persistent and important phenomenon in southern elections. Southern white voters—and southern white Republican voters—selecting Democratic nominees in black majority districts is obviously contrary to the spirit of the Voting Rights Act, and clearly an issue that African Americans in the South are going to be troubled by for the foreseeable future.

The strong Republican trends in federal officeholding in the South are now being matched at the state level. There are now seven Republican governors in the 11 southern states, and Republicans control 10 of 22 southern state legislative bodies. The strong growth in the numbers of black state legislators seen in the 1990s is now being replaced with a strong growth in the number of southern black state legislators serving in the minority. This obviously is a great concern to those committed to the fair representation of African Americans in the South. African Americans in the South and elsewhere still do not view the Republican Party as a viable alternative for their votes, and until this changes, Republican victories will mean diminished black representation.

Finally, an analysis of the available statistical evidence leaves unanswered the question of what size black population is necessary to ensure that black voters are able to elect the candidates of their choice. This is perhaps the most uncertain—and troublesome—issue of the post-2002 political environment.

NOTES

1 Interestingly, southerners are stronger in the Republican Party than the Republican Party is in the South, which is two-party competitive. In several southern states the Democratic Party is more powerful than the Republican Party.

2 V.O. Key, *Southern Politics in State and Nation* (New York: Alfred A. Knopf, 1950).

3 Texas, which is in the border South, was an exception; the black-white vote difference was 65 percentage points (91 vs. 24 percent). However, Texas is Bush's home state, which likely explains the discrepancy.

4 The Hispanic voting-age population was not statistically significant in the model.

5 This was a stepwise regression with incumbency status explaining 58.3 percent of the variance on the first step, and BVAP contributing an additional 16.7 percent. For the variable incumbency, black incumbents are coded "1," black candidates running in open seat districts are coded "0," and black candidates facing white incumbents are coded "-1."

6 Of course, in a district with a 36.6 percent BVAP, the chances of a black candidate becoming the Democratic nominee (assuming a black candidate is the preferred choice of the black voters in the district) depends upon the primary's field of candidates. If such a contest featured one white candidate and two black candidates, the white candidate's prospects would be significantly improved. In some places in the country, e.g., St. Louis, the white political and economic leadership, or some faction of that leadership, have been predisposed to recruit and financially support a second black candidate for the purpose of diminishing the chances of the first.

7 Former U.S. Representative Cleo Fields (D-LA) decided not to seek re-election (after two terms in congress) after a federal court redrew the Louisiana map (U.S. House districts) and reduced his district to a 27.3 percent BVAP.

8 In the South, Democratic candidates running for statewide office rely upon black voters for a much greater share of their vote-up to (and occasionally over) 50 percent.

9 V.O. Key, *Politics, Parties and Pressure Groups*, 5th ed. (New York: Thomas Y. Crowell, 1964).

10 See David A. Bositis, *Blacks and the 2000 Republican National Convention* and *Blacks and the 2000 Democratic National Convention* (Washington, DC: Joint Center for Political and Economic Studies, 2000).

11 At the present time, a few black Republicans have risen to higher party leadership position. However, this tends to be in states with comparatively large minority populations and where the Republican Party is weak, for example, California and Maryland.

12 In a 1999 Joint Center national survey of black elected officials, 14 percent identified themselves as Republican and 76 percent identified themselves as Democrats (See *Changing of the Guard: Generational Differences Among Black Elected Officials* [Washington, DC: Joint Center for Political and Economic Studies, 2001]).

13 The practical consequence of this is that the choices African Americans face are between voting for Democrats or not voting. The second option is regrettably the choice of many African Americans (See David Bositis, *The Political Perspectives of Young African Americans* [Washington, DC: Joint Center for Political and Economic Studies, 2001]).

14 A legal challenge to the crossover voting has been filed in the U.S. District Court, Northern District of Georgia by five black voters in the district. The case is *Osburn,*

DuBose, Clemons, Perry, and Muhammed v. State of Georgia, Sonny Purdue (Governor of Georgia), Cathy Cox (Secretary of State of Georgia), Dekalb and Gwinnett County Boards of Elections and Registration, Linda Latimore (Dekalb Supervisor of Elections), Lynn Ledford (Gwinnett Supervisor of Elections), and the Georgia Democratic Party.

15 Many cities with African American majorities, including Washington, DC, have had mayoral elections where white voters have determined which of two (or more) black candidates was elected.

16 The measure of racial diversity used here is the variation ratio, which is simply the proportion of the population in a district outside the modal category for the district. A district that is racially homogenous, i.e., all voters are black, Hispanic, or white, will score zero on the variation ratio, since 100 percent of the cases are in the modal category. With race (simplified) taking three categories here (black, Hispanic, and white), the most racially heterogenous district would have a voting-age population that was one-third black, one-third Hispanic, and one-third white, and thus, the modal category would contain one-third of the population-and the variation ratio will take on a maximum value of 0.67.

17 Republicans control both legislative chambers in Florida, South Carolina, Texas, and Virginia, two southern states are now split, Georgia and North Carolina, and in the remaining southern states the Democrats control both legislative chambers.

Figure 3.1. 2000 Presidential Vote by Race and State, Black Voting-Age Population: Southern States

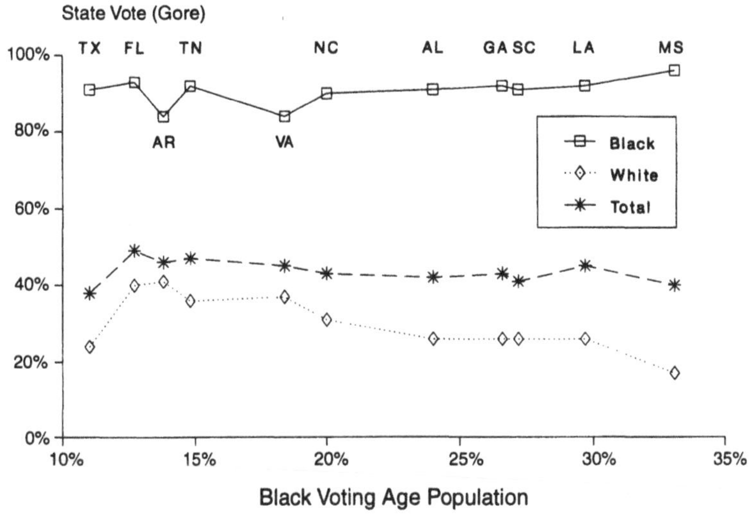

Figure 3.2. McKinney Vote by Black Vote Share, Precinct-Level Data

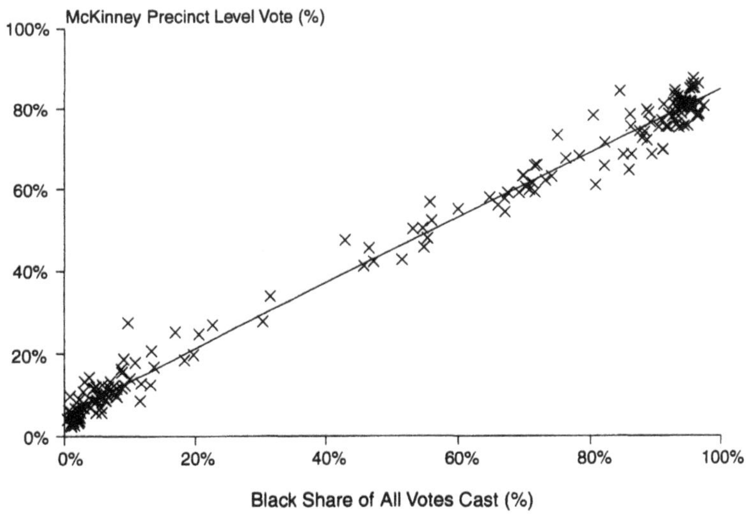

Figure 3.3. Majette Vote by White Vote Share, Precinct-Level Data

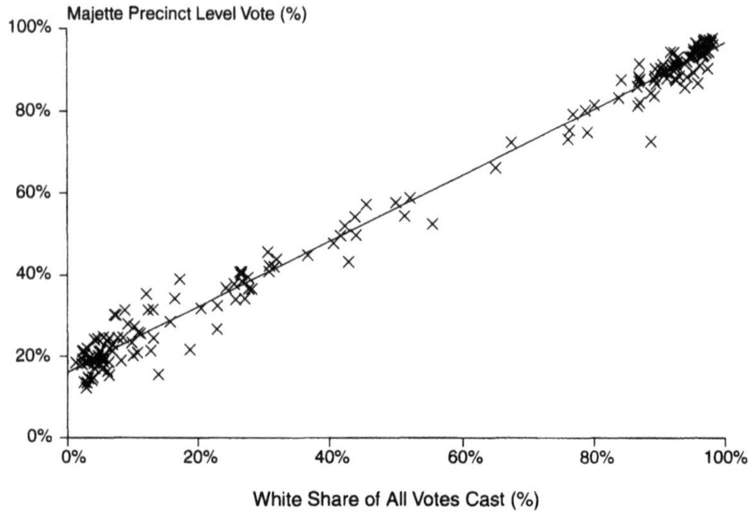

Figure 3.4a. Before Reapportionment: 102nd Congress

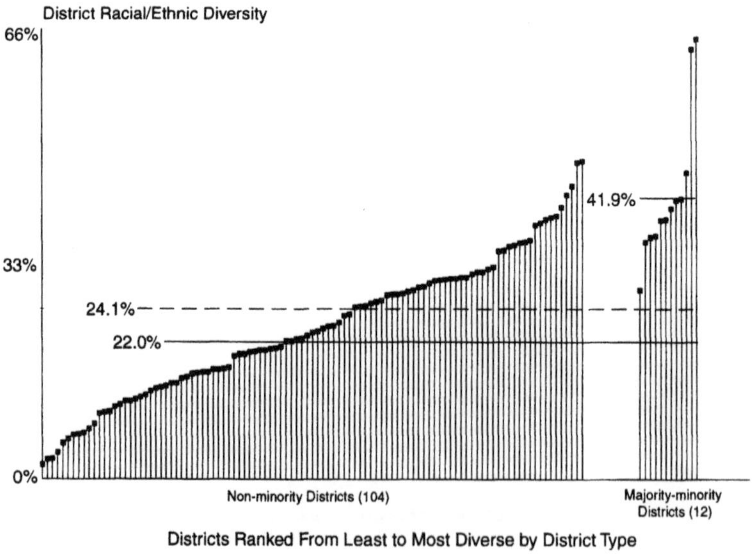

Figure 3.4b. After Reapportionment: 103rd Congress

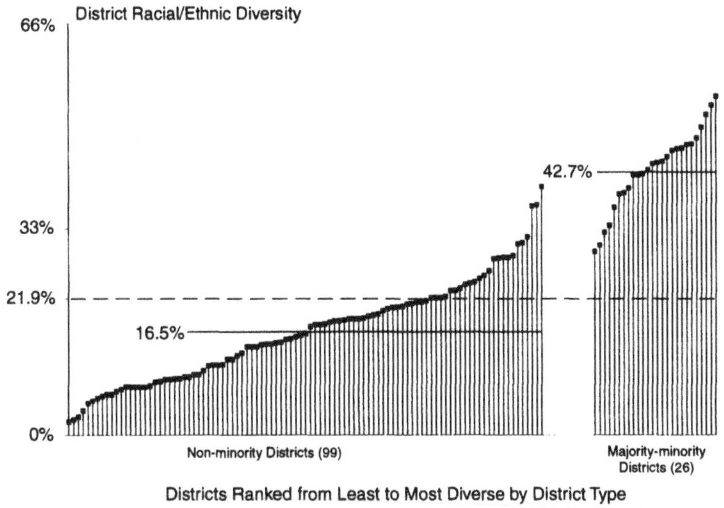

Figure 3.5a. Before Reapportionment, 107th Congress (2000)

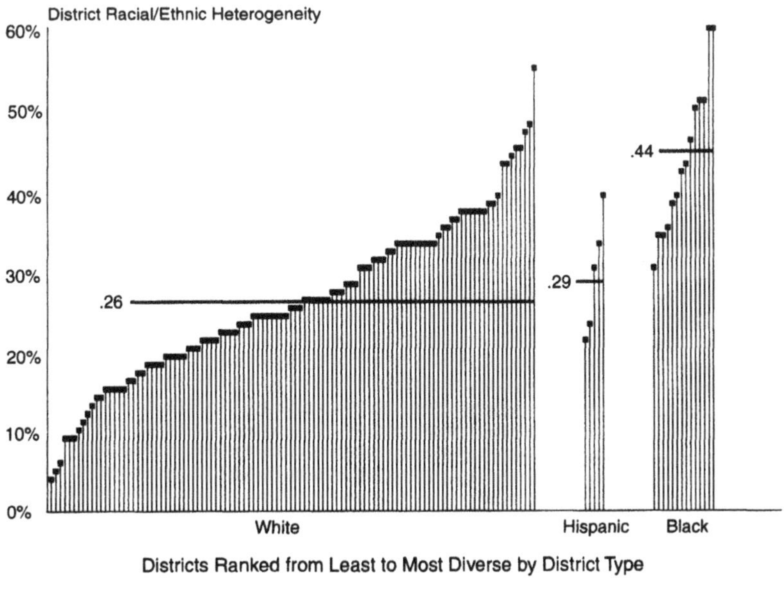

Figure 3.5b. After Reapportionment: 108th Congress (2000)

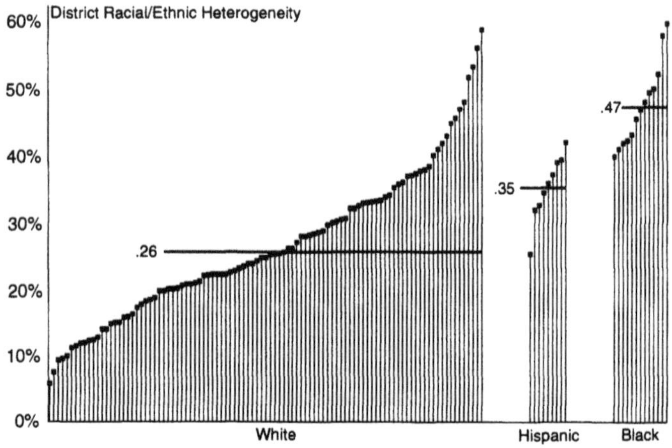

Districts Ranked from Least to Most Diverse by District Type

Figure 3.6. Percent of Black Voters Residing in U.S. House Districts Represented by CBC Members 102nd - 107th Congress

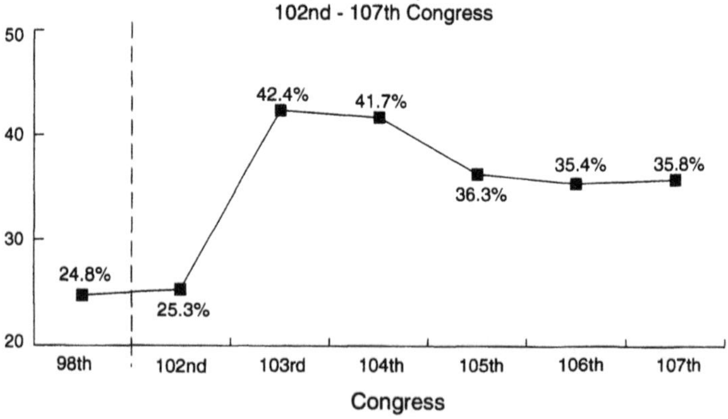

Table 3.1
Black v. White U.S. House Candidates, Southern States, 1990–2000

Year	District	BVAP(%)	HVAP(%)	Black Candidate	White Candidate	Black Candidate Vote	White Candidate Vote
1990							
	MS 4	41.2	0.4	Jerry Parks (R)	√Mike Parker	19	80
	TN 9	59.3	0.7	√Harold Ford	Alan Davis	65	35
1992							
	FL 3	50.6	2.8	Corrine Brown	Don Weidner	59	41
	FL 23	45.7	9.4	Alcee Hastings	Ed Fielding	59	31
	GA 2	52.3	1.7	Sanford Bishop	Jim Dudley	64	36
	GA 5	57.2	1.8	√John Lewis	Paul Stabler	72	28
	GA 11	60.4	1.1	Cynthia McKinney	Woodrow Lovett	73	27
	LA 4	62.6	0.9	Cleo Fields	Charles Jones	74	26
	NC 1	53.4	0.7	Eva Clayton	Ted Tyler	67	31
	SC 6	58.3	0.8	James Clyburn	John Chase	65	35
	TN 9	54.1	0.7	√Harold Ford	Charles Black	58	28
	TX 18	43.5	15.3	Craig Washington	Edward Blum	65	33
	TX 29	9.8	60.6	Clark Ervin (R)	Gene Green	35	65
1994							
	GA-2	52.3	1.7	√Sanford Bishop	John Clayton	66	34
	GA-5	57.2	1.8	√John Lewis	Dale Dixon	69	31
	GA-11	60.4	1.1	√Cynthia McKinney	Woodrow Lovett	66	34
	NC-1	53.4	0.7	√Eva Clayton	Ted Tyler	61	39
	NC-12	53.3	0.9	√Mel Watt	Joe Martino	66	34
	SC-6	58.3	0.8	√James Clyburn	Gary McLeod	63	36
	VA-3	61.2	1.4	√Robert Scott	Tom Ward	79	21
1996							
	AR 4	23.7	0.8	Vincent Tolliver	√Jay Dickey	36	54
	AL 7	63.5	0.3	√Earl Hilliard	Joe Powell	71	27
	FL 3	42.3	2.8	√Corrine Brown	Preston Fields	61	39
	FL 23	45.7	9.4	√Alcee Hastings	Robert P. Brown	73	27
	GA 2	35.1	1.7	√Sanford Bishop	Darrel Ealum	54	46
	GA 4	32.8	1.2	√Cynthia McKinney	John Mitnick	58	42
	MS 4	36.5	0.4	Kevin Antoine	Mike Parker	36	62
	NC 1	53.4	0.8	√Eva Clayton	Ted Tyler	66	33
	NC 12	32.6	0.8	√Mel Watt	Joe Martino	71	27
	SC 6	58.3	0.8	√James Clyburn	Gary McLeod	68	30
	TX 18	43.5	20.8	Sheila J. Lee	Larry White	77	10
	TX 30	42.4	16.1	Eddie B. Johnson	John Hendry	55	18
1998							
	GA 2	35.1	1.7	√Sanford Bishop	Joseph McCormick	57	43
	NC 1	46.5	0.7	√Eva Clayton	Ted Tyler	62	37
	NC 12	32.6	0.3	√Mel Watt	Scott Keadle	56	42
	SC 6	58.3	0.8	√James Clyburn	Gary McLeod	72	26
	TN 9	54.1	0.7	√Harold Ford, Jr.	Claude Burdikoff	79	19

Table 3.1, cont'd.
Black v. White U.S. House Candidates, Southern States, 1990–2000

Year	District	BVAP(%)	BVAP(%)	Black Candidate	White Candidate	Black Candidate Vote	White Candidate Vote
	TX 30	41.8	17.1	√Eddie B. Johnson	Carrie Kelleher	70	29
2000							
	FL 23	55.3	13.1	√Alcee Hastings	Bill Lambert	76	24
	GA 5	62.9	5.1	√John Lewis	Hark Schwab	78	22
	MS 2	65.2	1.2	√Bennie Thompson	Hardy Caraway	65	31
	NC 1	50.5	3.1	√Eva Clayton	Duane Kratzer, Jr.	66	33
	NC 4	19.8	3.4	Jess Ward (R)	√David Price	37	62
	NC 12	44.5	6.8	√Mel Watt	Chad Mitchell	65	33
	SC 3	20.9	1.8	George Brightharp	√Lindsay Graham	30	68
	TX 18	40.4	33.5	√Sheila J. Lee	Bob Levy	77	22
	VA 1	19.5	2.8	Lawrence Davies	Jo Ann Davis	37	58
	VA 5	24.0	1.6	John Boyd, Jr.	√Virgil Goode (I)	31	67

√ = Incumbent.

Note: All black candidates not identified as Republicans are Democrats.

Sources: 1990 and 2000 population figures are Census counts from those years; Other year totals are from "1990 Census Population and Housing Profile: Congressional Districts of the 103rd Congress," except for post-1996 figures from Florida, Georgia, North Carolina, Texas, and Virginia, whose districts were reconfigured due to successful court challenges to the original districts. Candidates and election results are from the Joint Center's "Blacks and the 1990-2000 Elections" series.

4. Drawing Effective Minority Districts: A Conceptual Model

Lisa Handley

When the U.S. Supreme Court held in *Shaw v. Reno* (1993) that districts drawn predominantly on the basis of race violated the Equal Protection Clause of the Fourteenth Amendment, many feared the decision would precipitate a dramatic reduction in the number of minorities elected to office. While the decision did spawn a number of lawsuits (most of them successful) and the reconfiguration of numerous legislative districts, many with minority percentages less than 50 percent, the predicted decrease in minority representation did not materialize. The reason for this is that minority candidates often do not need districts that are majority-minority in composition to win. In fact, the percentage of the population that needs to be minority to elect minority-preferred candidates to office varies from jurisdiction to jurisdiction. Sometimes minority-preferred candidates can easily be elected from districts that are less than 50 percent minority; sometimes significantly more than 50 percent minority may be required to provide minorities with an opportunity to elect candidates of choice.

Presented herein is a model for estimating the percentage of minority population needed to provide minority voters with an opportunity to elect their preferred candidates. This model is then applied to actual election outcomes in several jurisdictions.[1]

Court-Dismantled Congressional Districts

A number of the majority-black districts that elected African Americans to Congress in 1992 and 1994 were later dismantled when the U.S. Supreme Court held, in a series of cases beginning in 1993 with *Shaw v. Reno*,[2] that districts drawn predominantly on the basis of race violated the Equal Protection Clause. Over the course of the decade, courts ordered the redrawing of nine majority-black congressional districts in six southern states: Florida, Georgia, Louisiana, North Carolina, Texas, and Virginia.[3] The black population concentrations in eight of these nine districts fell below 50 percent black.[4] Despite the substantial decrease in the number of black voters, African American incumbents in all of these districts, except Cleo Fields in Louisiana's Fourth District, sought re-election in the newly configured districts, and contrary to the expectations of many, all proved successful in their bid for re-election.

Table 4.1 (see tables at end of chapter) lists the election results for seven of the eight districts that were redrawn with less than majority-black populations as a result of successful court challenges. (The Fourth District is not included in the table because the black incumbent did not seek re-election, and no other black candidate ran in the reconfigured district.)

Why did these black incumbents continue to win despite having to run from districts that were no longer majority-black? Did the level of racially polarized voting decrease over the course of the decade—that is, were whites more likely to vote for black candidates in 1996 and 1998 than they were in 1992 or 1994? Or was it because these African American candidates had the benefit of being the incumbents in these districts? In fact, there is little evidence to support either of these contentions.

An examination of voting patterns in these districts indicates pronounced racial bloc voting in these elections: Almost all black voters cast a ballot for the African American candidate, while only about a third of the white voters voted for the African American candidate.[5] This pattern appears to be stable over the course of the decade, with the average percentage of white voters casting their vote for black candidates in the general election only varying by one percentage point (34.1 to 35.1) between 1992 and 1998. Furthermore, only one black candidate, Rep. James Clyburn in South Carolina's Sixth District, appears to have clearly benefited among white voters from his incumbency status. Reps. Corrine Brown and Melvin Watt showed sporadic increases in white support, but Reps. Eva Clayton and Cynthia McKinney appear to have actually lost white support since their first election in 1992.[6]

If these African American representatives did not succeed because whites had become more willing to vote for them—either because they were simply more willing to vote for black candidates in general or because these black candidates were incumbents—how is it they have continued to win? The simple answer is that these black candidates may not have needed super-majority black congressional districts to win in the first place, at least as long as they ran in districts without a white incumbent.[7]

Estimating the Minority Percentage Needed to Elect Minority-Preferred Candidates

The likelihood of electing a minority-preferred candidate to office depends on several factors: the relative rate at which minorities and whites participate in the electoral process, the degree to which minority and white voters support minority-preferred candidates, and the presence of a two- or three-stage electoral process that includes a primary, a general election, and, in some instances, a runoff election. To determine the racial composition necessary to provide minorities with an opportunity to elect minority-preferred candidates, all of these factors must be considered.

Of course, while we can estimate participation rates and support for minority-preferred candidates from previous elections, we must be sensitive to context since a number of factors can affect the ability of minorities to elect minority-preferred candidates. Perhaps the most important of these is the presence of an incumbent in the district; for instance, the presence of an entrenched white incumbent will make it more difficult for a minority-preferred candidate to win, but a popular minority incumbent may decrease the minority percentage necessary to elect minority-preferred candidates. Other factors include the availability of experienced minority candidates and campaign organizers, minority access to campaign funding, and the number (and minority status) of the candidates who choose to run for office in the district. Other potential complications with calculating the percentage of minority population required to produce an effective district include the presence of military bases, universities, or colleges—military personnel and students are often registered to vote elsewhere—as well as the number of geriatric homes and prisons.

Equalizing Minority and White Turnout

Minorities usually require more than a simple majority in a district if they are to comprise 50 percent of the voters on election day. There are several reasons for this: (1) the voting-age population is typically a lower proportion of the total population among minorities than among whites; (2) registration rates are often lower for minorities; and (3) turnout rates are usually lower for minorities than for whites. Thus, even if minorities constitute 50 percent of the overall population in a district, they often do not make up 50 percent of the voters casting ballots on election day.[8]

To ascertain the percentage of minority population necessary to ensure an equal number of minority and white voters turning out to vote, the first step is to calculate the proportion of each population that turns out to vote. Obviously, if a smaller proportion of the minority population is turning out than is true for the white population, then whites will make up a higher proportion of the voters if the minority population is only equal to (and does not exceed) the white total population in a given district.

The second step is to calculate the percentage of minority population necessary to equalize minority and white turnout. The equalizing percentage is calculated mathematically by solving the following equation:

Let

M = *the proportion of the district's total population that is minority*

$W = 1\text{-}M$ = *the proportion of the district's total population that is white*

A = *the proportion of the minority population that turned out to vote*

B = *the proportion of the white population that turned out to vote*

Therefore,

(1) $M(A)$ = *the proportion of total population that is minority and turned out to vote*

(2) $(1\text{-}M)B$ = *the proportion of total population that is white and turned out to vote*

We want to find out what value of M is needed for (1) and (2) to be equal. Algebraically, we set them as equal and solve for M:

$$
\begin{aligned}
M(A) &= (1 - M)B \\
M(A) &= B - M(B) \\
M(A) + M(B) &= B \\
M(A + B) &= B \\
M &= B/A{+}B
\end{aligned}
$$

Thus, for example, if 57.8 percent of the minority population turned out and 68.6 percent of the white population turned out, the percentage of minority population needed to equalize minority and white turnout would be 54.3 percent [M = .686/(.686 + .578) = .5427)].

Utilizing Charles Bullock and Richard Dunn's estimates of the percentages of black and white registered voters who turned out to vote, the percentage of black registered voters needed to equalize black and white turnout in a number of southern congressional districts was calculated.[9] These estimates are listed in Table 4.2.

In almost all of the districts listed, whites turned out at higher rates than blacks in the general elections examined; hence, the percentage of black population needed to equalize black and white turnout was greater than 50 percent in most of these districts.[10]

Incorporating Cohesion and Crossover Voting into the Model

The phrase "effective voting equality" has been used in the past to mean the percentage of the population that must be minority to yield an expected equality of minority and white turnout on election day.[11] But equalizing minority and white turnout is not sufficient to ensure that minority voters will have an equal opportunity to elect minority candidates. It is also necessary to incorporate the level of minority cohesion and the degree of white crossover voting that can be expected when a minority-preferred candidate competes for office. If minority voters are not voting cohesively for a single preferred candidate, this can increase the percentage of minority population necessary to create an effective district. On the other hand, if white voters are regularly crossing over to vote for minority candidates in substantial numbers, this will decrease the percentage minority necessary to create an effective minority district.

An analysis of voting patterns conducted over a series of elections can be used to generate the expected minority vote for minority-preferred candidates (minority "cohesiveness"), and the expected white crossover vote for the minority-preferred candidates. Expected levels of minority cohesion and white crossover can then be taken into account when determining the percentage of minority population required to give minority voters the opportunity to elect candidates of choice.

If an examination of a number of elections shows, for example, that a minority candidate can expect, on average, 85 percent of the minority votes and 20 percent of the white votes and the average white turnout rate is 45 percent and the average minority turnout rate is 40 percent, the estimated support for the minority-preferred candidates would be calculated as follows:

Support for minority-preferred candidate =

minority support for minority-preferred candidate	+	*white support for minority-preferred candidate*
(.40 x .85)	+	*(.45 x .20)*

Estimated support for the candidate not preferred by minorities would be:

Support for candidate not preferred =

minority support for other candidate	+	*white support for other candidate*
(.40 x .15)		*(.45 x .80)*

The percentage of minority population needed for the minority-preferred candidate to win would then be based on the following calculation:

$$\frac{\text{Support for non-minority candidate}}{\text{Support for non-minority candidate} + \text{support for minority candidate}}$$

$$\frac{(.06 + .36)}{(.06 + .36) + (.34 + .09)}$$
$$= .494$$

Any district greater than 49.4 percent minority in this specific area should provide minority voters with an opportunity to elect minority-preferred candidates to office.

Listed in Table 4.3 are calculations of the percentage of black registered voters needed for a black candidate to have an equal opportunity to win (that is, receive 50 percent of the vote) in the general election in each of the districts studied by Bullock and Dunn. Estimates of black and white participation rates and the percentage of black and white voters casting votes for the African American candidate in these districts are from Bullock and Dunn.[12]

The estimates for the percentage of black population necessary for black-preferred candidates to win the general election, given relative levels of participation and given the degree of black cohesion and white crossover voting, is less than 50 percent in every instance and in most cases is in the range of 33 to 39 percent. This is because even though blacks typically turn out to vote at lower rates than do whites, blacks vote very cohesively—over 95 percent of the black voters consistently voted for the black Democrat in a general election—and approximately one-third of the white voters supported the black Democrat in the general election.

Incorporating the Primary and Runoff Elections Into the Model

In the United States, a candidate often must compete in and win a primary election—and sometimes a runoff election as well—before proceeding to the general election. The presence of multiple stages in the election process should not be ignored in calculating the percentage of minority population needed to create an effective minority district.

The percentage of black registered voters needed to win the Democratic primary and the Democratic runoff, again based on estimates of black and white voting behavior reported by Bullock and Dunn, is displayed in Table 4.4.[13]

As this table demonstrates, the percentage of black population needed to win is usually considerably lower in the Democratic primary than the percentage needed to win in the general election.[14] But the highest percentage is not always found in the general election. Sometimes the runoff requires a higher percentage to elect the black-preferred candidate. Both Reps. Sanford Bishop and Cynthia McKinney (Georgia Second and Georgia Eleventh), for example, needed a higher percentage of black population to win the Democratic runoff than to win the general election in their districts in 1992.

It is always the highest of the two or three percentages that is important, because this is the percentage needed for the black-preferred candidate to win all elections—the Democratic primary, the Democratic runoff, and the general election—to attain a seat in the legislature. The fact that the highest percentage minority needed to create an effective district is not always found in the general election demonstrates the importance of examining all stages of the election process, rather than simply relying on an analysis of the general election to reach this determination.

Applying the Model: Effective Minority Districts in the 2000 Round of Redistricting

The model outlined in this paper can be used to determine whether a proposed redistricting plan, and more specifically certain minority districts within the proposed plan, offer minority voters an opportunity to elect candidates of choice. For example, this model was employed by the author in a number of states to assist in ascertaining if proposed minority districts drawn following the 2000 Census met the requirements of the Voting Rights Act. (This model was used in conjunction with a variety of other approaches that have not been discussed in this paper.) Included is a brief discussion of two states in which this model was used: Alaska and Arizona.

Alaska

Background. Section 5 of the Voting Rights Act of 1965 requires all jurisdictions covered by this section of the act to preclear any changes in their electoral laws, including the enactment of a redistricting plan, with the U.S. Department of Justice before the change can be implemented. To obtain preclearance, a covered jurisdiction must establish that the voting change "does not have the purpose and will not have the effect of denying or abridging the right to vote on account of race, color, or membership in a language minority group."[15]

Because Alaska is a jurisdiction covered by Section 5, the state is required to submit its redistricting plans for preclearance before they can be implemented. The burden of proof rests with the state to demonstrate that the plan does not result in a retrogression of minority voting strength relative to the current, or benchmark, redistricting plan.[16]

The 1990s state legislative plan for the state of Alaska—the benchmark plan—contained six effective Alaskan Native house districts: four that were majority Alaskan Native (House Districts 36, 37, 38, and 39) and two that were approximately 30 percent and 34 percent Alaskan Native in voting-age population but consistently elected minority-preferred Alaskan Natives to the legislature (House Districts 5 and 40). In the state senate, there were two majority Alaskan Native districts (Senate Districts S and T), both of which elected Alaskan Natives to the state senate, and an additional senate district that was 36 percent Alaskan Native and consistently elected a minority-preferred Alaskan Native to office (Senate District R).

The Alaska Redistricting Board's 2000 state legislative plan also contained four majority Alaskan Native house districts (House Districts 6, 38, 39, and 40), as well as two additional effective Alaskan Native districts (House Districts 5 and 37). The state senate plan maintained two majority Alaskan Native senate districts (Senate Districts S and T) and an additional effective Alaskan Native senate district (Senate District C) that was 43 percent Alaskan Native in voting-age population.

Table 4.5 provides a comparison of the effective minority districts in the 1990s state legislature to the effective minority districts in the new plan. The numbering system for the legislative districts changed, so districts that are in approximately the same area of the state have been compared in the table.

The new plan maintains the same number of minority districts, and all but one of the new districts have approximately the same or a higher percent Alaskan Native as the comparable district in the old plan.

One district, however, lost Native population relative to the benchmark plan. House District 6—which was House District 36 in the old plan—went from 63.2 percent Alaskan Native to 51.7 percent Alaskan Native in voting-age population. To ascertain whether this decrease in Native population was retrogressive, an analysis of Native and non-Native turnout rates and Native and non-Native votes for the Native-preferred candidate between 1994 and 2000 was conducted, with a focus on the specific area in question.[17]

Equalizing Turnout. In Alaska, minority turnout is *not* generally lower than white turnout. In fact, Alaskan Native turnout was almost always higher than non-Native turnout in the elections examined. The estimates of turnout (as a percentage of voting-age population) for the general election contests examined between 1996 and 2000 are listed in Table 4.6.

The statewide pattern of higher Native than non-Native turnout held for House District 36 specifically. The average percent Native turnout in House District 36 is 47 percent, based on estimates for general elections since 1994. The average percent non-Native turnout in House District 36 is 44.1 percent, based on estimates for general elections since 1994. The percent Native needed to equalize turnout in this area of Alaska is therefore 48.4 percent.

Incorporating Cohesion and Crossover Model. An analysis of voting patterns by race in general elections in Alaska indicated that minority-preferred candidates can expect approximately one-third of the white vote in a general election. This is a sizable amount of white crossover for minority-preferred candidates; in fact, crossover rates this high usually mean that majority-minority districts may not be required to provide minority voters with the opportunity to elect minority candidates.

Looking specifically at House District 36, the average percent of Alaskan Native voters voting for the Native-preferred candidate since 1994 is 63.8 percent and the average percent of non-Native voters voting for the Native-preferred candidate since 1994 is 35.9 percent. The estimated percentage of support for Native-preferred candidates is therefore 45.8 percent:

Support for Native-preferred candidate =

Native support for Native-preferred candidate	+ *non-Native support for Native-preferred candidate*
(.47 x .638)	+ *(.441 x .359)*

And the estimated proportion of support for the candidate not preferred by Natives is 45.3 percent:

Support for candidate not preferred =

Native support for other candidate	+ *non-Native support for Native-preferred*
(.47 x .362)	+ *(.441 x .641)*

The percent Native population needed for the Native preferred candidate to win is 49.7 percent based on the following calculation:

$$\frac{\textit{Support for non-Native candidate}}{\textit{Support for non-Native candidate} + \textit{support for Native candidate}}$$

$$= \frac{.453}{.453 + .458}$$

$$= .497$$

Any district greater than 49.7 percent Native in this specific area of the state should be an effective district. Proposed District 6, at 51.7 percent Alaskan Native, should therefore be sufficient to provide Native voters with an opportunity to elect Native-preferred candidates to state legislative office.

Conclusion. The Department of Justice did, in fact, determine that the state legislative plan passed by the Alaska Redistricting Board was not retrogressive, despite the decrease in the percentage Alaska Native population in one of the districts, and precleared the plan.

Arizona

Background. The State of Arizona, like the state of Alaska, is covered by Section 5 of the Voting Rights Act. Therefore, when the Arizona Independent Redistricting Commission redrew state legislative districts following the 2000 Census, the redistricting plan (the state house and state senate districts are identical) was submitted to the Department of Justice for preclearance. The benchmark plan—the 1990s Arizona state legislative plan—used by the Justice Department to determine if the proposed legislative plan was retrogressive included one majority Native American district (District 3), which was 74.6 percent Native American in total population and 70.5 percent Native American in voting-age population.

The legislative plan adopted by the Arizona Redistricting Commission also included a new majority Native American district, District 2, in the same general area as the old majority Native American district. The new district was 68.1 percent Native American in total population and 62.2 percent Native American in voting-age population. An analysis of participation rates and voting patterns by race indicates that this minority district, despite the decrease in percentage Native American, will continue to offer Native Americans an opportunity to elect candidates of choice. Because primary as well as general election results were available, this determination is based on an examination of both sets of elections.

Primary Elections. Turning first to the Democratic primary (the partisan primary election in which the vast majority of Native Americans participate), the second and third columns in the upper half of Table 4.7 list estimates of turnout by race in the area of the new Native American district. In this region of the state, Native American turnout far exceeded white turnout in recent elections; whites simply did not turn out to vote in the Democratic primary.

The degree of Native American cohesiveness and the degree of white crossover voting, given the enormous difference in turnout rates, are essentially irrelevant in the primary. Native American voters will control the Democratic primary regardless of the voting behavior of the few whites that do participate in the Democratic primary. As a consequence, a district with much less than a majority Native American voting-age population will produce a win for the Native American-preferred candidate in the Democratic primary in this area of the state.

General Elections. Based on voting patterns in recent general elections, Native Americans need much less than a majority Native American district to elect their preferred candidate in the general election as well. The average turnout rate of Native Americans has been almost twice as high as that of whites in recent general elections (see the second and third columns in the lower half of Table 4. 7). In addition, the average degree of Native American cohesiveness in general elections is very high, 79.9 percent (see column 5 of row labeled "average for general" in Table 4.7). And the average percent of white voters supporting the Native American-preferred candidate is far from negligible; an average of 27.2 percent of the whites supported the Native-preferred candidate in recent general elections (see column 6 of row labeled "average for general" in Table 4.7).

Of course, it is possible that the large differences in turnout are at least partially due to a lack of interest on the part of white voters, since this district was not competitive for non-Democrats (i.e., Republicans). Although District 2 has essentially the same Republican percentage as the old majority Native district (20 percent compared to 19 percent), it has more registered voters who have not declared a party. However, even if the difference in turnout were to diminish substantially, Native American-preferred candidates would still be likely to win the district. The row labeled "scenario #1" in the table posits the following scenario: maintaining current levels of cohesion and crossover, what percentage of Native American population would be needed for the Native American-preferred candidate to win if Native American and white turnout levels were equal? The answer: a 43.3 percent Native American voting-age population would produce a district that offers an equal opportunity for the Native American-preferred candidate to win the election.

The fact that there are fewer Democrats in District 2 than in the old Native district might decrease the expected white crossover vote. In the row labeled "scenario #2," equal turnout rates and a white crossover vote that is much less than average (a rate of only 10 percent white crossover vote in support of the minority-preferred candidate) are posited. Under these conditions, a 57.2 percent Native American district would be sufficient for the Native American-preferred candidate to win the election. Since the new majority Native American district is slighter over 62 percent Native, this district should offer Native Americans voters an opportunity to elect candidates of choice under either of these scenarios.

Conclusion. The Department of Justice, provided with evidence that a decrease in Native American population from 70 percent to 62 percent would not affect the ability of Native Americans to elect Native American-preferred candidates, declined to object to the plan in this region of the state. The proposed state legislative plan was not precleared, however; the Justice Department objected to the proposed plan's treatment of Hispanic voters.

Jurisdiction-Specific Analysis Is Key

There is no simple 50 percent cutoff point—or any other percentage—at which minority voters can be said to have an equal opportunity to elect candidates of choice. A functional analysis that is jurisdiction-specific, taking into account such factors as the relative participation rates for whites and minorities, degree of cohesion, and usual rate of crossover voting, as well as the multi-stage election process, must be conducted in order to determine the percentage minority necessary to create an effective minority district. Of course, context-specific factors other than those incorporated in our conceptual framework must also be considered in determining whether a district offers minority voters an opportunity to elect minority-preferred candidates to office, the most important being whether the district includes an incumbent or not, and if so, whether the incumbent is the minority-preferred candidate.

NOTES

1 This model has been outlined in previous articles, beginning with Kimball Brace, Bernard Grofman, Lisa Handley, and Richard Niemi, "Minority Voting Equality: The 65 Percent Rule in Theory and Practice," *Law and Policy* 10 (1, 1988) and most recently in Bernard Grofman, Lisa Handley, and David Lublin, "Drawing Effective Minority Districts: A Conceptual Framework and Some Empirical Evidence," *North Carolina Law Review* 79 (5, 2001).

2 *Shaw* v. *Reno*, 509 U.S. 630 (1993).

3 Florida: *Johnson v. Mortham*, 915 F. Supp. 1529 (N.D. Fla. 1995); Georgia: *Miller v. Johnson*, 115 S.Ct. 2475 (1995); Louisiana: *Hays v. State of Louisiana*, 839 F. Supp. 1188 (W.D. La. 1993); North Carolina: *Shaw v. Reno*, 113 S.Ct. 2816 (1993); Texas: *Bush v. Vera*, 116 S.Ct. 1941 (1996); and Virginia: *Moon v. Meadows*, 952 F. Supp. 1141 (E.D. Va. 1997).

4 The black populations in the Florida Third, the Georgia Second, and Eleventh, the Louisiana Fourth, the North Carolina First and Twelfth, and the Texas Eighteenth and Thirtieth fell below 50 percent. The Virginia Third went from 64 percent to 54 percent black when it was redrawn.

5 Charles Bullock and Richard Dunn, "The Demise of Racial Redistricting and the Future of Black Representation," *Emory Law Journal* 48 (1999). Of course, the actual percentage of the white vote received by each of the black candidates varied individually, but it was very unusual for a black candidate to receive majority support from whites. The only black congressional candidate to receive a majority of the white vote appeared to be Bobby Scott (Third Congressional District in Virginia), in 1992 and possibly 1994.

6 Bullock and Dunn, "The Demise of Racial Redistricting."

7 Evidence for this contention can be found in the large margin of victories by which these black candidates won office when their districts were still majority black; in Georgia, for example, Sanford Bishop won 64 percent of the vote in 1992 and 66 percent of the vote in 1994, and Cynthia McKinney won 73 percent of the vote in 1992 and 66 percent of the vote in 1994.

8 Brace et al., "Minority Voting Equality."

9 Bullock and Dunn, "The Demise of Racial Redistricting."

10 The only exception to this is the 1992 general election for the Eleventh Congressional District in Georgia, where over 60 percent of the blacks registered to vote cast a ballot compared to a little less than 58 percent of the whites. As a result, the equalization percent for this particular contest is slightly less than 50 percent (48.9 percent).

11 Brace et al., "Minority Voting Equality."

12 Bullock and Dunn, "The Demise of Racial Redistricting."

13 Bullock and Dunn, "The Demise of Racial Redistricting." There are far fewer elections listed in this table than in the previous tables because in many instances black incumbents did not face a primary challenge—and with the exception of 1992, did not face runoff elections at all—and estimates on black and white participation and voting patterns were not reported by Bullock and Dunn in a number of instances when the black incumbent did have an opponent in the Democratic primary.

14 The black percentage of population needed to win for the Democratic primary is somewhat misleading if more than one black candidate ran in the primary—the estimates for the percentage of whites crossing over and the percentage of blacks voting cohesively are a reflection of the percentage of whites and blacks voting for any of the black candidates, not simply the winning black candidate. For example, in the 1992 Democratic primary in the Georgia Eleventh, 60.4 percent of the whites voted for one of the four black candidates running, but not necessarily the black candidate (Cynthia McKinney) who won.

15 Four minority groups are protected under Section 5 of the Voting Rights Act: blacks, Hispanics, Native Americans and Alaska Natives, and Asians.

16 The benchmark redistricting plan against which a proposed plan is compared is the last legally enforceable plan (inevitably the redistricting plan currently in place) with the demographics of the 2000 Census data associated with the districts of this plan.

17 Due to the lack of primary election data available for analysis, primary elections could not be examined for the state of Alaska.

Table 4.1
Election Results for Eight Southern Congressional Districts Redrawn by Court Order

	Percent Black Population (1992)	First Election After Redraw	Percent Black Population After Redraw	Representative Elected After Redraw (All Black Incumbents)	Percent Vote Received
Florida 3	55	1996	47	Corrine Brown	61
Georgia 2	57	1996	39	Sanford Bishop	54
Georgia 11; 4	64	1996	37	Cynthia McKinney	58
North Carolina 1	57	1998	50	Eva Clayton	62
North Carolina 12	57	1998	36	Melvin Watt	56
Texas 18	51	1996	45	Sheila Jackson Lee	77
Texas 30	50	1996	45	Eddie Bernice Johnson	55
Virginia 3	64	1998	54	Bobby Scott	76

Table 4.2
Percent Black Registration Needed to Equalize Black and White Turnout: Select Southern Congressional Districts, General Elections 1992-1998

Congressional District	Year	Percent Black Participation	Percent White Participation	Percent Black Population Needed to Equalize Turnout
Florida 3	1992	57.8	68.6	54.3
Georgia 2	1992	55.9	62.6	52.8
Georgia 11	1992	60.3	57.8	48.9
South Carolina 6	1992	63.2	78.3	55.3
Georgia 2	1994	38.7	47.3	55.0
Georgia 11	1994	39.0	49.1	55.7
North Carolina 1	1994	36.0	44.8	55.4
North Carolina 12	1994	32.0	38.4	54.5
South Carolina 6	1994	48.4	64.6	57.2
Florida 3	1996	49.4	59.1	54.5
Georgia 2	1996	42.3	58.3	58.0
Georgia 4	1996	58.3	66.4	53.2
North Carolina 1	1996	45.4	56.2	55.3
North Carolina 12	1996	49.0	55.3	53.0
South Carolina 6	1996	54.3	63.7	54.0
Georgia 2	1998	37.8	42.9	53.2
Georgia 4	1998	45.6	50.5	52.5
North Carolina 1	1998	38.1	41.6	52.2
North Carolina 12	1998	35.7	42.4	54.3
South Carolina 6	1998	46.4	51.2	52.5

Table 4.3
Percent Black Registration Needed for Black-Preferred Candidate to Win, Incorporating Cohesion and Crossover: Select Southern Congressional Districts, General Elections 1992-1998

Congressional District	Year	Percent Black Participation	Percent White Participation	Percent Black Votes for Black Candidate (Cohesion)	Percent White Votes for Black Candidate (Crossover)	Percent Black Needed to Win
Florida 3	1992	57.8	68.6	97.1	25.6	41.7
Georgia 2	1992	55.9	62.6	98.3	32.4	36.5
Georgia 11	1992	60.3	57.8	96.7	36.0	33.0
South Carolina 6	1992	63.2	78.3	97.7	24.2	43.0
Georgia 2	1994	38.7	47.3	96.7	40.4	34.3
Georgia 11	1994	39.0	49.1	96.4	29.3	41.0
North Carolina 1	1994	36.0	44.8	97.1	30.6	39.8
North Carolina 12	1994	32.0	38.4	98.7	32.9	37.2
South Carolina 6	1994	48.4	64.6	97.3	27.7	42.5
Florida 3	1996	49.4	59.1	98.2	36.9	35.2
Georgia 2	1996	42.3	58.3	98.4	37.2	37.1
Georgia 4	1996	58.3	66.4	98.1	31.2	37.5
North Carolina 1	1996	45.4	56.2	98.9	30.3	39.0
North Carolina 12	1996	49.0	55.3	99.1	37.1	33.8
South Carolina 6	1996	54.3	63.7	97.3	31.9	38.0
Georgia 2	1998	37.8	42.9	97.9	39.5	33.1
Georgia 4	1998	45.6	50.5	95.1	36.0	36.0
North Carolina 1	1998	38.1	41.6	98.3	30.2	37.2
North Carolina 12	1998	35.7	42.4	98.9	34.0	36.3
South Carolina 6	1998	46.4	51.2	98.9	33.3	35.5

Table 4.4
Percent Black Registration Needed for Black-Preferred Candidate to Win in Select Southern Congressional Districts: Primary, Runoff, and General Elections 1992

Congressional District	1992 Democratic Primary	1992 Democratic Runoff	1992 General Election	Highest Percentage Needed to Win
Florida 3	31.9	36.7	41.7	41.7
Georgia 2	43.7	45.7	36.5	45.7
Georgia 11	27.4	49.3	33.0	49.3

Table 4.5
Comparison for Alaska Between Effective Minority Districts in 1990s and 2000 State Legislative Plan

Effective Minority Districts in 1990s Plan	Percent Alaskan Native	Comparable Districts in 2000 Plan	Percent Alaskan Native
State House Districts			
District 5	33.8	District 5	35.5
District 36	63.2	District 6	51.7
District 37	74.0	District 40	73.1
District 38	80.6	District 39	79.7
District 39	75.8	District 38	81.1
District 40	30.6	District 37	38.6
State Senate Districts			
R	35.9	C	42.5
S	77.3	T	76.4
T	55.3	S	57.5

Table 4.6
Turnout Rates for Alaskan Natives and Non-Natives in General Elections, 1996–2000

Alaska State Legislative District, by Election	Alaskan Native Turnout (% of voting-age population)	Non-Native Turnout (% of voting-age population)
2000 General Election		
House District 5	53.2	45.7
House District 36	46.4	51.0
1998 General Election		
House District 36	48.3	42.1
House District 39	43.8	24.9
Senate District R	46.4	45.1
Senate District T	45.0	13.9
1996 General Election		
House District 5	54.2	45.6
House District 36	46.1	40.9
House District 39	43.1	28.2
Senate District C	51.2	39.6

Table 4.7
Percent Native Voting-Age Population Needed for
Native-Preferred Candidate to Win:
Arizona State Legislative Elections (Legislative District 3), 1996–2000

Election Year and District	Percent Native Turnout	Percent White Turnout	Percent Native Needed to Equalize Turnout	Percent Native Vote for Native Candidate (Cohesion)	Percent White Vote for Native Candidate (Crossover)	Percer Native Neede to Wir
Democratic Primaries						
2000 Senate 3	22.8	.7		51.3	28.2	
2000 House 3	14.8	1.2		52.7	9.0	
1998 Senate 3	12.7	.1		47.4	100.0	
1998 House 3	1.1	.1		38.4	36.7	
1996 Senate 3	26.7	.2		78.8	44.9	
1996 House 3	20.8	.6		39.1	24.3	
Average for Primary	***16.5***	***.5***	***2.9***	***51.3***	***40.5***	***17.8***
General Elections						
2000 Senate 3	Uncontested					
2000 House 3	Uncontested					
1998 Senate 3	37.2	21.5		83.3	25.1	
1998 House 3	21.4	15.6		70.6	19.9	
1996 Senate 3	66.4	27.1		85.6	36.6	
1996 House 3	Uncontested					
Average for General	***41.7***	***21.4***	***33.9***	***79.9***	***27.2***	***28.1***
Scenario # 1	20.0	20.0	50.0	79.9	27.2	43.3
Scenario #2	20.0	20.0	50.0	79.9	10.0	57.2

5. Redistricting 2000: A Lost Opportunity for Latinos

Leo F. Estrada

At the beginning of the decade, political analysts expected that Latinos would experience greater gains in congressional representation than any other group from the reapportionment and redistricting following the 2000 Census. There was every reason to be optimistic. Throughout the decade, Census Bureau estimates signaled that Latino growth would be impressive due to a combination of high fertility and continued immigration. In 2001, when the Census Bureau released its official figures, Latino leaders had every reason to be elated. The census figure of 35.3 million exceeded the Census Bureau's own official estimates by 3.5 million. A population that added 13 million more Latinos over the decade had to expect that it would advance its national political representation.[1]

Yet, despite these phenomenal gains in population, it now appears that a combination of circumstances will prevent Latinos from realizing their hopes for greater political representation during this redistricting cycle. Some of these circumstances stem from the demographic profile of the Latino population, including population dispersal and low rates of eligibility, citizenship, and political participation. While these factors played a role, the actions of the political establishment also contributed to Latinos' failure to attain clout commensurate with their numbers. The failure of politicians to understand the dimensions and implications of the demographic shift, their perception that Latinos could not exact political reprisals, fear of violating "race as a predominant factor" proscriptions, and structured ethnic-racial competition all contributed to less-than-expected gains for Latinos.

A Decade of Demographic Growth

The Latino population grew by 58 percent in the 1990s, as compared with just 8.7 percent growth over the decade for the non-Latino population. Thus,

Latinos, who comprise 13 percent of the national population, accounted for 65 percent of the nation's population growth in the 1990s. These are rather remarkable and impressive numbers. Considering that redistricting is based on population totals, many assumed that this enormous population increase would mean that Latinos would attain several goals:

- More districts with significant numbers of Latino constituents and greater visibility of Latinos within these districts;
- More districts with Latino-majority populations with an opportunity to elect candidates of their choice;
- More influence in local and state elections; and
- Greater representation in state legislatures and the U.S. Congress.

Although Latinos did realize gains in all these areas, they were much less significant than had been anticipated by many based on Latino population growth.

Population Dispersal

Although redistricting rewards population growth, it also requires that population groups be residentially concentrated in order to draw majority-minority districts. Latino growth in the 1990s did in fact increase the density of Latinos in the states in which they have traditionally been concentrated: California, Texas, New York, Florida, Illinois, Arizona, and New Jersey. In 2000, two states, California and Texas, still accounted for half of the U.S. Latino population—31 percent and 19 percent, respectively. Further, three states with traditionally large Latino populations—California, Texas, and Florida—accounted for about half of the total growth of 13 million Latinos.

Latino population growth in the 1990s, however, expanded beyond the states that had served for decades as ports of entry for Latino immigration. Among the states with impressive gains in Latino population were states in the South and Midwest that had not previously been thought of as immigration destinations for Latinos: North Carolina (+394%), Arkansas (+337%), Georgia (+300%), Tennessee (+278%), Nevada (+217%), South Carolina (+211%), Alabama (+208%), Kentucky (+173%), Minnesota (+166%), and Nebraska (+155%). (See Figure 5.1.)

The dispersal of the Latino population was generally attributed to the search for employment opportunities in agriculture, food processing, construction, and various service industries. This was particularly true in areas where the proportion of the population that was of working age declined. Further fueling this dispersal were high demand for low-paid service workers and recruitment of craft workers by certain industry sectors.

The seven million Latinos who reside outside the top ten Latino states typically live in metropolitan areas that offer them limited opportunities for electoral influence. In metropolitan areas, Latino influence is typically restricted to the areas in which they are residentially concentrated. In addition, many other groups are competing for political representation. The exception, however, is the growing electoral influence Latinos are exerting in small rural towns across the United States, where their numbers impact local politics quickly because of the simultaneous decline of the older white population in these areas.

Thus, the impressive growth of the Latino population was offset to some extent by its dispersal outside the most populous Latino states. Also, Latinos in metropolitan areas moved from their traditional ethnic enclaves into suburban areas, further fragmenting the population.

The Benefits of Reapportionment

The reapportionment process also seemed likely to favor advances in Latino political representation. Three states with large concentrations of Latinos—Arizona, Florida, and Texas—gained two additional congressional seats. Two other states with significant Latino populations, California and Colorado, each gained one additional congressional seat. Among the nine states losing congressional seats, in only two states—Illinois, which lost one congressional seat, and New York, which lost two congressional seats—were Latino opportunities at risk as a result. As indicated below, existing Latino congressional districts were not challenged in Illinois or New York; thus, the net gain from reapportionment was six new congressional seats in densely Latino states.

Eligibility and Citizenship

An analysis of achievements in Latino electoral representation cannot ignore the issues of eligibility and citizenship. As indicated in Table 5.1, Hispanics obtain approximately 16 votes for every 100 persons in the population, compared to approximately 46 votes for every 100 persons in the white, non-Latino population. As illustrated in the table, Latinos have several disadvantages in creating a strong electoral presence:

- Latinos are younger on average and thus a higher proportion of Latinos are too young to vote;
- The number of Latino noncitizens is sizeable and thus a very high proportion of Latinos are ineligible to vote;
- Latinos' voter registration rates are the lowest of all groups'. Generally speaking, voting rates increase with age, education, income, employment rates, and home ownership;
- Latinos are younger than the general population and have lower incomes and lower rates of educational attainment and home ownership.

In time, the Latino population will begin to mature. With that maturity and greater educational attainment, their levels of employment, income, and home ownership will increase. Until that time, the size of the Latino population will not translate into commensurate voting power.

One positive sign is the higher-than-average rates of voting for newly naturalized citizens. The U.S. Census Bureau reports that voter turnout in the 2000 election was 49.6 percent for naturalized citizens, compared to 43.6 percent for U.S.-born Latinos.[2] With 4.1 million Latino naturalized citizens and millions more ultimately eligible for naturalization, Latino electoral strength can be accelerated through greater efforts to register newly naturalized citizens.

2000 Redistricting Results

The redistricting process is not yet complete. Some states are still considering competing plans while other states are in litigation over their plans. While the final outcome is still in doubt, at this point it is expected that Latinos will increase their representation in the U.S. Congress from 19 to 22 members, a disappointingly small gain for adding 13 million to their ranks. The following state-by-state analysis reflects the situation at the end of 2002.

Texas

In the decade of the 1990s, Texas grew by 3.8 million persons, 60 percent of whom were Latinos. The 2000 Census reported 6.7 million Latinos living in

Texas, making them nearly a third (32 ent)perc of the state's total population. Based on that growth, it was expected that Latinos would have an opportunity to gain two additional congressional seats. Texas was among the first states to redistrict, and it set the tone for what was to come. The legislature failed to consider redistricting legislation, and the task passed to the Texas Legislative Redistricting Board, which created a status quo plan. The Mexican-American Legal Defense and Education Fund (MALDEF) sued the redistricting board.[3] A panel of three U.S. District Court judges ruled partly in favor of the plaintiffs and redrew the state house districts to add one more Latino-majority district. Latinos now hold 30 of Texas's 150 state house seats and 7 senate seats out of 31. However, the courts let stand the redistricting board's congressional plans. Thus, Latino growth in Texas did not result in any additional seats to the six already held in the U.S. House of Representatives.

Despite the lack of increase in majority-Latino congressional seats, Texas elections will be closely watched over the coming decade. The recent election, which included a slate with an African American candidate for the U.S. Senate (former Dallas mayor Ron Kirk) and a Latino businessman for governor (Tony Sanchez), energized voter registration among minority populations.

New York

In the 1990s, New York grew by 986,000 persons, 66 percent of whom were Latinos. Latinos comprise 2.9 million or 15 percent of the state's population and continue to be concentrated in the greater New York metropolitan area. Unlike other states with large concentrations of Latinos that experienced high rates of growth in the Latino population, New York lost two congressional seats in the apportionment process following the 2000 Census. To accommodate this change, congressional districts in upstate New York were collapsed. Thus, Latinos retained their two congressional seats (Rep. Jose Serrano and Rep. Nydia Velazquez) out of the state's 29-member congressional delegation. Latinos retained the four seats they have in the 61-seat state senate and saw an increase from eight to 13 representatives in the state house, which has a total of 150 seats.

Florida

In the 1990s, Florida grew by 3 million persons, and Latinos accounted for 36 percent of this increase. The 2000 census counted 2.7 million Latinos, representing 17 percent of the state's total population. Florida's Latinos continue to be concentrated in the southernmost part of the state, particularly Dade and Broward counties. Unlike most Latinos, Florida's Cuban Americans mostly favor Republican candidates; their demographic profile (education, age, income) also varies considerably from that of other U.S. Latinos.

With two new congressional seats, the GOP-dominated Florida legislature created a new Republican-leaning congressional district (District 25), which elected Mario Diaz-Balart, a man whose brother, Rep. Lincoln Diaz-Balart, is currently serving in Congress. Latino congressional representation from Florida will increase by one, to three out of 25. Latinos retained the three seats they held in the 40-seat state senate and increased their representation from 12 to 13 in the 120-member state house.

Illinois

Over the 1990s, Illinois grew by 989,000 persons, 63 percent of whom were Latinos. In 2000, Illinois' 1.5 million Latinos comprised 12 percent of the state's population but were largely concentrated in the Chicago metropolitan area. Due to reapportionment, Illinois lost one congressional district. The state legislature originally created four majority-Latino state house seats, two majority Latino state senate seats, and one congressional seat. Latino groups organized to advocate additional Latino majority seats, and in the end the state legislature added more Latino districts. This plan, benefiting Latino representation, was challenged by two lawsuits.[4] As a result, MALDEF has entered the fray as a defendant-intervener to protect the state legislative plan. In November 2001, the Illinois Supreme Court upheld the legislative plan. Thus, Latinos hold six of 118 state assembly seats and four of the 59 state senate seats. They also will retain the fourth congressional seat held by Rep. Luis Gutierrez. One of the achievements of this recently enacted plan is the creation of six Latino-majority assembly districts outside the city of Chicago.

California

California grew by 4.1 million persons; Latinos accounted for 80 percent of that increase. In 2000, Latino population in the state stood at an impressive 11 million, representing nearly a third (32 percent) of the state's population; Latinos remained concentrated in the southern part of the state, particularly Los

Angeles County. Despite efforts by several groups to influence the state legislative redistricting process, the governor and state legislative leaders agreed beforehand to create a status quo plan that would retain the same numbers of Democratic and Republican legislative seats as in 1990. To do so required that the Latino population be concentrated in Latino districts and, in several cases, be fragmented to dilute Latino voting strength. As a result, Latinos hold 16 of 80 seats in the state assembly and seven of 40 seats in the state senate.

When the state legislature failed to include a new congressional seat in the San Fernando Valley, which has a Latino population of more than 800,000, MALDEF sued.[5] This challenge has received some press coverage because it focuses on two congressional districts held by Congressmen Berman and Sherman, who previously have had support from Latinos for their pro-Latino political stances. The data show that one of the two districts could have been configured to be an effective Latino majority seat. But rather than jeopardize the incumbency of either of these popular congressmen, the state legislature chose to fragment the Latino population. The federal courts upheld the state redistricting plan, and the U.S. Supreme Court concurred. Latino congressional representation from California will increase by one with the addition of labor leader Linda Sanchez in a heavily Democratic district in southeast Los Angeles County. Sanchez is the sister of current Congresswoman Loretta Sanchez. Latinos will hold seven of 53 California congressional seats.

Arizona

The 2000 Census counted 1.3 million Latinos in Arizona, which makes them one quarter of the state's total population. Reapportionment added two more congressional seats, and the new District 7 in Tucson was won by a Latino businessman and former Pima County Board of Supervisor, Raul Grijalva. Thus Rep. Ed Pastor has a new Latino colleague in Congress. Latinos retained their five seats in the 30-seat state senate and increased their representation in the 60-seat state house from nine to ten.

New Mexico

The 2000 Census counted 765,400 Latinos in New Mexico, making them 42 percent of the state's population. As of the fall of 2002, New Mexico was the only state with five statewide Latino elected officials—Governor Bill

Richardson, Secretary of State Rebecca Vigil-Giron, Attorney General Patricia Madrid, State Auditor Domingo Martinez, and State Treasurer Robert Vigil. Currently, Latinos do not hold a congressional seat in the state; however, they have retained their hold on 15 seats in the state senate out of a total of 42 seats. Latinos lost one seat in the state house but still hold 30 seats out of 70 state house seats.

New Jersey

In 2000, the census counted 1.1 million Latinos in New Jersey, which made them 13 percent of the state's population. The current District 13 Congressman, Rep. Robert Menendez, will continue to represent his district and remain the sole Latino representing the state's 13 congressional districts. Latinos hold no seats in the state senate and retain the seven seats they hold in the 80-member state house.

Other Accomplishments

Several other political milestones were attained:

- The first Latino (Sam Zamarripa) to serve in Georgia's state senate;
- The first two Latinos (David Casas and Pedro Marin) to serve in Georgia's state house;
- The first two Latinos (Victor Ramirez and Ana Sol Gutierrez) to serve in Maryland's House of Delegates;
- The first Latino (Jarrett Barrios) to serve in Massachusetts' state senate; and
- The first Latina (Susan Castillo) to be elected statewide in Oregon (Superintendent of Public Instruction).

Analysis

Even at this point, it is clear that the expectations for some quantum leap in Latino political power based on the 2000 Census will not be fulfilled. The reapportionment process gave high-density Latino states six new congressional opportunities. Latinos will take three of those six new seats-one new congressional seat each in Arizona, California, and Florida. This is clearly an advance, but one that pales in terms of the 13 million person increase in population. How does one explain this outcome? There are a number of reasons why expectations have not been met.

Demographic Denial

Despite the phenomenal growth of the Latino population over the last two decades, legislative decision-makers have largely ignored the implications of the demographic shift. National decision-makers still perceive Latinos as regional minorities and relegate their issues to those areas with high Latino concentrations. The reality, however, is that given current trends, Latinos will be one of every six persons in 2020 and one of every four persons by 2050.

The ambiguity found in both political parties is illustrative. On the one hand, the political parties have stepped up efforts to attract Latino voters. These efforts, however, have not included integration of Latinos into the party leadership. They also have taken place while the parties have simultaneously bashed immigrants, reduced transnational exchange opportunities, and pushed aside youth-focused agendas. Political parties, worried about the next election, have appealed to their traditional base and ignored the changing demographic and political terrain. While they attend to the present, the political parties are not building the foundation they need for the future electorate.

The Race-as-a-Predominant-Factor Scare

The post-*Shaw* era heavily influenced the 2001 redistricting process. Legislators were alerted by their legal advisors that the redistricting process had to avoid the use of race "as a predominant factor." The warning was made so often that legislators began to act as if they could not consider race at all. Some legislators requested that analysis of race/ethnicity in developing redistricting plans be banned. More reasonable legislators understood that racial/ethnic data was an essential part of the process, yet were uncomfortable discussing topics such as racial/ethnic fragmentation or ability-to-elect in public hearings. Because legislators became so paranoid that comments on race would be misconstrued, the discussion of race and ethnicity in the redistricting process was stifled in public hearings.

Ethnic-Racial Competition

Discussion of increased representation for Latinos was often cast as a zero-sum game, thus creating ethnic/racial tension. The assumption was that Latino gains could only be attained by reducing African American representation or denying Asians opportunities for representation. The truth is that African American elected officials are more likely to have Latino constituents than vice versa. African Americans in Latino areas have been able to retain their districts with the support of white and Latino voters. There are areas where tensions exist, such as Chicago, New York, Houston, and Dade County, Florida. There are more examples where Latinos and African Americans often work together, including Dallas, Oakland, San Diego, Newark, and San Antonio. Latinos in Los Angeles, for example, protested to the U.S. Department of Justice about the dilution of African American districts for the state legislature. Likewise, Asians often represent Latino and African American populations; for example Assemblywoman Judy Chu (Monterrey, CA) represents a majority Latino district while Assemblywoman Wilma Chan (Oakland, CA) represents a mixed African American-Latino majority district. In many parts of the country, racial/ethnic groups are coming to the realization that representation by elected officials not of one's own group can be a uniting force rather than a divisive one.

No Fear of Reprisals

Above all, legislators perceive Latinos as a weak electorate—uninvolved and unable to make them pay a price for acting to protect incumbents rather than expanding opportunities for Latino representation. Without fear of reprisal, state legislatures refused to create more minority districts and wielded their power to protect incumbents. In most cases, they had the support of Latino legislators to protect them. State redistricting in California, Texas, and New Mexico were highly disrespectful acts toward the Latino community that show the degree to which legislative leaders felt they could act with impunity.

A Failure of Political Influence

Redistricting requires legal analysis, demographic and technical skills, and political influence. In the most recent redistricting process, considerable attention was given to compliance with the legal post-*Shaw* decision requirements. Technological advances made the demographic-technical aspect more accessible and opened up the redistricting process to more groups. But in the end, a well-configured legal map must have "political legs" to influence the process.

Latinos in 2002 had the technical ability to participate in the process and the legal resources to create technically competent maps that met all the legal requirements. However, they lacked the political backing in state legislatures to have their plans considered, particularly when increased Latino representation came at the expense of incumbents. Advances in Latino representation in Congress came from states that obtained additional seats from reapportionment.

In these states, Latino gains were possible because they did not threaten incumbents.

Perhaps most disturbing is that the redistricting plans adopted by state legislatures have structured competition between Latinos and non-Latino incumbents. With most districts configured to be safe seats, Latinos can only increase their representation over the next decade by challenging incumbents. Challenges are inevitable since Latino Democratic voters were typically used to buttress Democratic districts. Latino candidates capable of attracting cross-ethnic votes will begin to challenge incumbents in the next election cycle.

Political parties take a risk by ignoring Latino representation. Future population projections indicate that the number of new voters, either through aging or naturalization, will increase the Latino electorate exponentially. While Latinos do not have a church infrastructure similar to that of African Americans to promote civic participation and voting, they do have a national Spanish language media capable of mobilizing them. With a deep immigrant experience, Latinos and Asian Americans have commonalities that could lead to a powerful coalition in several parts of the United States. Despite the outcome of this most recent redistricting, their numbers will eventually mean that Latinos will gain greater control over their political destiny.

NOTES

1 All numbers not otherwise referenced are derived from the 2000 Census. For state population totals by race and Hispanic origin relevant to redistricting, go to www.census.gov/clo.www/redistricting.html.

2 U.S. Bureau of the Census, "Voting and Registration in the Elections of November: 1996-2000" (Washington, DC: Government Printing Office, 2001).

3 *Balderas v. Texas Civil* No. 6:01-CV-158 (E.D. Tex), *aff'd* No. 01-1196 (U.S. June 17, 2002).

4 *Campuzano v. Illinois State Board of Elections* alleged that the Illinois redistricting map was not compact, not politically fair, and violated the Voting Rights Act. (*Campuzano v. Illinois State Board of Elections* No. 01 C 50376 [N.D. Ill. May 3, 2002]. *Cole-Randazzo v. Ryan* alleged that the Illinois plan was not sufficiently compact *Cole-Randazzo v. Ryan* 762 N.E. 2d 485 [Ill. 2001]).

5 In *Cano v. Gray Davis*, plaintiffs argue that the core Latino community was fragmented to allow two incumbents to retain their seats. Congressional District (CD) 28 was 65.5 percent Latino (38.5% voter registration) and CD 26 (renumbered) is now 55.7 percent Latino (27% voter registration). The adjoining district siphoned off Latinos. CD 27 was 8.1 percent Latino. Under the new configuration, CD 27 became 17.8 percent Latino. *Cano v. Gray Davis* 193 F. Supp. 2d 1177 (CD Cal 2002).

Table 5.1
Translating Population into Electoral Power:
Voter Impact per 100 Population

	White Non-Hispanic	Voter Impact/100	Hispanic	Voter Impact/100
Total Population	192,253	100	36,288	100
Population 18+/Pop	148,035	77	23,587	65
Noncitizens 18+	3,303	75	8,440	42
Eligible 18+ Pop	144,732		15,147	
Registered to Vote	103,588	54	7,546	21
Reported Voting	89,469	46	5,934	16

Source: Current Population Survey, *Voting and Registration, Election of November 2000,* (P20-542)

6. Reapportionment/Redistricting Politics in Georgia in the 1990s and 2001-2002: Reflections of a Participant-Observer

Bob Holmes

The redistricting process is always a contentious one that makes enemies of friends and neighbors. While the redistricting battles in the Georgia legislature following the 1990 and 2000 censuses were as hotly fought as any in Georgia history, they also were dramatically different from those that preceded them. Much of this difference was fueled by the awareness among state Democrats that their unchallenged control of state politics was ebbing away. Since Reconstruction, Democrats had dominated both houses of the legislature and the governorship. In fact, Georgia had never elected a Republican governor. With growing support among white suburban voters, Republicans could see the prospect of political control of the state within their grasp. Within this dynamic, the Georgia Legislative Black Caucus (GLBC) was able to greatly expand its participation and exert greater influence than ever before.

The following discussion is based on my participation in those momentous events as a state legislator and member of the GLBC. Generally, the discussion includes an explanation of the major features of the 1990 and 2000 redistricting and reapportionment processes, with a special emphasis on how they differed from previous political struggles. I have examined the outcome of these legislative battles, the subsequent decisions of federal three-judge district courts, the results of the 2002 election, and the implications of these events for black politics in Georgia. My primary focus, however, is on the evolving role of the Georgia Legislative Black Caucus and the consequences for black political representation and influence.

Redistricting/Reapportionment After the Voting Rights Act

After passage of the Voting Rights Act of 1965, Georgia's legislature approved reapportionment/redistricting plans after each census that were designed to dilute African American voting strength. Rather than complying with the intent of the act and attempting to maximize the number of African American-majority congressional and state legislative districts, the General Assembly sought to minimize their number. Typically, the white Democratic leadership would draw plans over the protest and opposition of black legislators, who would then appeal to the U.S. Department of Justice (DOJ) to withhold preclearance of the plans. During the 1970s and 1980s, the assistant attorney general for civil rights refused to preclear any of Georgia's plans, which then ended up before the federal judiciary. In each instance, more majority-African American state legislative districts were required, and additional black legislators were subsequently elected.

Reapportionment/Redistricting in 1991-1992[1]

The 1991 special legislative session from August 19 to September 4, 1991, was similar to its predecessors in 1971 and 1981. The Republican Party expected to continue its pattern of gaining additional seats in the General Assembly based on the rapid growth of the Atlanta region and other suburban areas in the state, combined with the creation of additional majority-black districts. The state house and senate redistricting committees proposed plans with little input from the GLBC, which offered its own plans. For example, the house committee voted out a plan for 35 majority-black districts (28 existed), and the GLBC proposed a plan that created 42 majority-black districts. The senate committee adopted a plan sponsored by African American Senate Majority Leader Charles Walker that drew 10 majority-black districts, while the GLBC offered a plan for 13 majority-black districts. Two GLBC members, Representatives Cynthia McKinney and Tyrone Brooks, proposed a third plan, called "the max black," which created 51 majority-black house districts and 15 senate districts.

Congressional redistricting was the most controversial of the three plans as Georgia's population growth during the 1980s had resulted in a gain of one seat, increasing the state's representation from ten to eleven. With incumbent congressmen lobbying legislators incessantly, some meetings went as late as 3 a.m., before a plan was agreed upon with two majority-black districts, despite the GLBC's efforts to secure a third. The map shattered several incumbents' congressional districts, including that of Newt Gingrich, then Republican Minority Whip in the U.S. House of Representatives. Each plan split the districts of some GLBC members. Some of these GLBC members, along with black civic leaders, threatened to ask the Justice Department to deny preclearance and to bring suit in federal district court.

The Georgia General Assembly passed the plans adopted by their redistricting committees with 35 African American-majority districts in the house, 10 in the senate, and two in Congress. More than 30 black legislators and civic leaders took a bus to Washington, DC, to state their case to the Justice Department. But the State of Georgia was late sending its supporting documentation for the plan so DOJ did not send its objection to the plans until January 21, 1992, two weeks after the regular session of the Georgia legislature had convened. The assistant attorney general for civil rights said white Democrats had sought to minimize black voting strength and had refused to consider several alternative plans that would have created more majority-black districts. The Georgia house and senate reapportionment committees then created two majority-black congressional and one black-influence district (39.4 percent black voting age population [BVAP]) over the objections of several black legislators.

Again, the GLBC was divided in its support of the congressional and state legislative plans. A second delegation of black leaders met with Assistant Attorney General John Dunne and urged him to insist that a plan be drawn to create three majority-black congressional districts rather than two. The chairs of the Georgia senate and house reapportionment committees expressed disappointment at DOJ's earlier decision, but they implored the Georgia General Assembly to address the concerns mentioned.

The senate adopted its revised plan after adding two new districts and creating a plan with 12 majority-black districts. Two of the districts had black majorities of 50.7 percent, and black majorities increased in four districts represented by incumbent GLBC members. The house adopted a plan that created 38 majority-black districts, including three with no incumbents and eight with an increased black percentage. Representative Brooks, along with several other GLBC members, voted against the plan and vowed to ask the Justice Department to object to it.

The congressional plan was far more difficult to draw and adopt. The senate and house passed different plans, and a conference committee was appointed to resolve the differences. Speaker of the House Murphy angered the GLBC and north Georgia legislators by appointing south Georgians to all three slots on the committee. The house plan created two majority-black districts, but several GLBC members had drafted and submitted separate plans for a third district. The conferees recommended and the house and senate adopted the two majority-minority district congressional plan. However, Representative Brooks said the plan was worse than the one sent to Washington in 1991 and that the Justice Department would reject it.

Both sides again journeyed to Washington to meet with DOJ officials to plead their cases on all three plans. Dunne reiterated the same concerns as in his previous rejection of the state plans, that the legislature had continued to "fragment and submerge" the black electorate, particularly in southwest and central Georgia, in an attempt to ensure the re-election of white incumbent legislators. The response to Dunne's continued rejection of the General Assembly's redistricting plans was mixed. Conference committee members expressed "disappointment," while several GLBC members were "ecstatic" and called the DOJ action a "landmark decision." Both the *Atlanta Constitution* and Lieutenant Governor Pierre Howard urged the General Assembly to deal with the maps quickly (five days remained in the legislature's annual 40-day session).

The reapportionment committees convened while other legislators adjourned for the weekend. After working late hours, on the thirty-seventh day near midnight, the senate created a plan that called for three majority-black senate districts, while the house adopted a plan for itself that created 41 majority-black districts, including a 59 percent black district for white Majority Leader Larry Walker. Again, the congressional plan proved to be problematic. General Assembly leaders accused the Justice Department of holding the state house and senate plans hostage in an attempt to force them to adopt a congressional plan with three majority-black districts. On the thirty-eighth day of the 40-day session, the Justice Department rejected the house plan. The house plan was revised again to create another majority-black district in the Columbus area and resubmitted to Washington.

At last, the conference committee adopted a controversial congressional plan with three majority-black districts. House Majority Whip Denmark Groover urged his colleagues to stand up to the DOJ and vote against the plan, which he said emasculated central Georgia. Representative Brooks also objected, saying the new plan continued to fragment and dilute the black vote; he called for larger black percentages in the districts. The American Civil Liberties Union said it was a decent plan and urged the DOJ to approve it.

Dunne approved all three plans. Representative Brooks said, "We got 98 percent of what we were fighting for: 41 state house, 13 senate and 3 majority-black congressional districts." However, the two chairs of the reapportionment committees were "not happy" about the plan, saying it might hurt blacks in some areas and that it had caused serious political pain for them and many colleagues. But this was not the final act in this long-running political play, which would continue through 1996.

The Legal Aftermath of 1991-1992[2]

The 1992 elections were held under the DOJ-approved plan mentioned above, and African Americans won in all three majority-black congressional districts. Five persons then filed suit in Rep. Cynthia McKinney's 11th District, including one defeated candidate who argued that the district was racially gerrymandered and violated the Equal Protection Clause of the Fourteenth Amendment to the U.S. Constitution. The southern federal district court ruled in the case of *Miller* v. *Johnson* (1995) that the 11th District was unconstitutional because race was the predominant factor in the adoption of the plan. The state did not defend the plan. Speaker Murphy and Lieutenant Governor Howard testified that the legislature was not attempting to remedy past discrimination (a compelling state interest), but was forced to draw the district to meet DOJ's demand that a "black maximization" policy be followed on all three plans. The U.S. Supreme Court ruled 5 to 4 against the plan because it said the Voting Rights Act did not require race-based redistricting or maximization of black representation.

Black leaders in Georgia feared the decision would result in a reversal of legislative gains made since enactment of the Voting Rights Act. Governor Zell Miller called a special session to address state and congressional reapportionment as well as other issues. Attorney Lee Parks threatened to file suits against the senate and house plans, saying they were racially gerrymandered. The GLBC was livid, and its chair appointed a task force on redistricting to meet with various legal and civil rights organizations and develop a strategy for the special session. Two weeks before the special session was to convene on August 14, the federal district court set a hearing date for August 22 and asked the litigants to submit their plans by August 15, along with their views on why the court should not draw the plan. Some observers speculated that the court intended to preempt the legislature's prerogative to draw the redistricting maps. Speaker Murphy attempted to use the court's August 2 order to get the GLBC to agree to a congressional plan lest the court draw one that would be even more detrimental to their interests. The GLBC had a planning retreat prior to the special session, from which it emerged with a slogan of "Three Seats, No Retreat."

While the focus was on the congressional plan, the Democratic leadership's primary agenda was state house and senate redistricting to protect powerful white committee chairs, party leaders, and allies of the speaker in the house and of the governor in the senate. Two days before the hearing date of August 22, neither the house nor the senate committees had drawn a congressional plan. Some said that they were content to let the court draw a congressional plan with one majority-black district, arguing it was not retrogressive because there was only one such district in the previously adopted 1981 plan. GLBC members broke ranks and began to negotiate to protect their individual districts. The senate plan introduced during the first week reduced the BVAP percentage of two majority-black districts then represented by white Democrats from 62 to 43 percent and 59 to 42 percent, while a third was decreased from 56 to 50 percent. Two white committee chairs were given more black Democrats in their districts to assist them in future races against Republican challengers.

In the house, nine formerly majority-black districts became majority-white to help the majority leader, governor's assistant, floor leader, and the chair of the Natural Resources and Environment Committee. The districts of two black legislators (Eugene Tillman and Carl Von Epps) also were reduced below 50 percent. Overall, 69 house districts were changed without any formal consultation by the house leadership with the GLBC. Republicans called it an assault on black and GOP districts and an attempt to reverse the results of the elections of the 1990s, which had seen an increase in both.

Speaker Murphy rejected an effort by some GLBC members to pair the congressional and house redistricting plans so neither would be voted on until there was agreement on both. A GLBC-Republican coalition blocked the house plan 89 to 87 (two short of a constitutional majority), with all 32 black members voting against the plan. It was believed that failure to pass this plan would enhance GLBC leverage with congressional redistricting and help protect black and congressional lawmakers. However, when Majority Leader Walker asked for reconsideration of the vote on the house plan, 26 of 32 GLBC members reversed their positions to reconsider the failed plan, and a modified version that made slight increases to the two black legislators' districts passed. A coalition of civil rights groups said the plan turned back the clock on African American voting rights and was vote dilution and retrogression. The president of the Georgia State Conference of NAACP chapters, Walter Butler, criticized the GLBC members who voted for the plan to reduce the number of black majority districts, saying their votes would make appeals to the DOJ and future litigation more difficult.

In the senate, the GLBC split over similar alleged dilution in black senate districts, with five voting for and five against the plan. GLBC member Senator Walker, chair of the Democratic Caucus, called the plan the best deal possible to preserve and protect black incumbents, but GLBC member Senator David Scott called it a "terrible mistake" and criticized Democrats for dismantling black majority districts and diluting the black vote.

One day before the August 22 federal court hearing date, the house passed a congressional plan with one majority-black district (Congressman Lewis) and two districts with approximately 40 percent BVAP (Bishop and McKinney). The plaintiff's attorney said blacks should form biracial coalitions to win election and warned that the court would draw the plan if this were not done. A GLBC task force drew a plan designed to gain the support of the white Democratic leadership; their plan contained two majority-black districts with 56.31 and 53.37 percent BVAP and a third with 49.5 percent. The plan passed 103 to 66 after a GOP-sponsored plan, identical to one submitted to the courts by Congressman Lewis and U.S. House Speaker Newt Gingrich, failed by a 62 to 108 vote. The house-adopted plan was submitted to the court as a status report. However, Senator Mark Taylor, Governor Miller's floor leader, offered a substitute plan to create one majority-black district. In a not-so-subtle racist appeal, Taylor urged his colleagues "to vote for the plan if they were tired of paying for the sins of their fathers and grandfathers." His plan put Congressman Bishop into a white GOP incumbent's district, which led GLBC member Senator Ed Harbison to call it "a deliberate attack against black congressmen." The Taylor plan passed with all 10 black senators voting against it.

The major differences between the house and senate plans meant a conference would find it difficult to adopt a plan that could be approved. The speaker of the Georgia house appointed a GLBC member, Rep. David Lucas, to the conference committee and said all three house members must agree on any plan before it would be brought to the floor for a vote. A civil rights coalition group composed of the Concerned Black Clergy, NAACP, Rainbow Coalition, and the SCLC condemned the senate action and white Democrats who supported it for emasculating the Voting Rights Act. They threatened to file a Section 2 lawsuit and ask DOJ to reject the plan under Section 5. In addition, other agendas had emerged. Some Democratic legislators were interested in putting Congressmen Newt Gingrich and Bob Barr in the same district. Several senate members wanted to create districts in which either they or their friends could run; others wanted to protect GOP incumbents. The GLBC feared white Democrats in the house might abandon them and accept a proposal similar to the senate plan. The senate adopted a resolution to adjourn the special session 30 to 21, with seven black members voting yes.

The session was bizarre. Some days started at 10 a.m. and ended at 1 a.m., punctuated by numerous two- and three-hour breaks to stand at ease pending the call of the chair. After these breaks, the session often would reconvene for two or three minutes, followed by another prolonged recess. One conference committee report was so bad that it was voted down 2 to 54 in the senate and only received 19 of 180 votes in the house. Factionalism was rampant among Republicans and between white and black Democrats. Rep. Gingrich urged GOP legislators to vote to adjourn the session, and a majority in the senate heeded his call. Georgia house members rejected his request publicly from the floor. Meanwhile, house GLBC members feared their white Democrat colleagues might join with dissident GOP senators to pass a redistricting plan, but their fear that the court might draw the plan was even greater. In such an atmosphere, tempers flared, deadlock ensued, and each side blamed the other for the stalemate. After a Sunday marathon session that ended at 10 p.m., the speaker of the Georgia house said the legislature should go home. After one more day of acrimonious negotiations, the house finally had enough and voted 102 to 50 to adjourn *sine die*, and the senate voted 40 to 13 to go home. Thus the legislature put congressional redistricting back into the hands of the court.

Reactions to this development were mixed. Gingrich and U.S. Rep. John Linder were pleased, while McKinney said it was a shame that the legislature threw in the towel. Bishop said the General Assembly did the best it could under the circumstances, but there were too many serious disagreements to reach a consensus. White Democrats believed that the judges would draw the districts to increase the opportunities to elect white Democrats to Congress. Finally, the black legislators were nearly unanimous in their fear that the senate version might have passed and felt the federal court might be a better place to draw the maps even after what happened in 1991-1992.

As noted earlier, the U.S. Supreme Court declared the congressional map with three majority-black districts unconstitutional. The federal district court then drew a plan that created only one black-majority house district. Lee Parks, who filed the plaintiffs suit in 1992, asserted that 17 state legislative majority-black districts had been drawn unconstitutionally, 12 in the house and five in the senate. The court said that in the interim, the 1995 plan would be used to hold the 1996 election, after which a permanent plan would be drawn to be used for the 1998 and 2000 elections. The court ordered the parties to meet with a mediator during the middle of the regular 1997 legislative session and reach an agreement before the General Assembly adjourned. Instead of changing 17 state districts, the legislature changed 45 (36 house and nine senate), which angered many legislators, but the General Assembly adopted the plan. It reduced the BVAP percentage in three majority-black house districts and one senate district to minority status for a total of 15 such reductions of majority-black districts since the 1991 maps were drawn. Both plans were enacted, bringing closure to the legislature's six-year odyssey to adopt acceptable state and congressional reapportionment/redistricting plans.

GLBC Struggles During 1990s Redistricting

The 1991 special session, 1992 regular session, and 1995 special session after the Supreme Court declared the Eleventh Congressional District unconstitutional were among the most intense, combative, and divisive for the GLBC in its history. The GLBC challenged the longest-tenured speaker in the nation over his maps and his appointment of three white rural legislators to the conference committee. Conference committee negotiations evoked charges of "racism" and "sell-out" and other personal attacks on legislators. The GLBC split into two factions over the issue of three versus two majority-minority congressional districts and the number of majority-black state house and senate seats that could be created.

The GLBC used a variety of strategies and techniques to increase the chances of electing African Americans to legislative seats, including:

- Negotiation with the white Democratic leadership
- Formulation of alternative redistricting/re-election plans
- Threats to appeal to the DOJ and file a lawsuit in federal court
- Voting with GOP legislators where their goals coincided, and
- Division of the GLBC into three segments ("Insiders," "Outsiders" and "Compromisers") to secure plans close to their objectives.

This approach worked in the political arena, but ultimately the courts overturned their political gains. Thus, as the 2000 Census approached, the prospects for a successful outcome in the forthcoming 2001 special session on redistricting/reapportionment were uncertain.

Redistricting/Reapportionment 2001-2002

The Georgia General Assembly convened in August 2001 to begin the reapportionment/redistricting process pursuant to the results of the 2000 census. Compared to the previous processes in 1981 and 1991 through 1996, this session was destined to be unique in many ways:

- Guidelines were different for the process.
- The governor played a major role for the first time in history.
- Black legislators were major players in drawing the legislative districts.
- There were multiple racial and partisan political agendas.
- Democratic performance, not black voter age population, was the major criterion used in drawing all three maps.
- Multimember districts were the major component of the Democrats' strategy with black support.
- The primary division was between Democrats and Republicans, not between black and white Democrats.
- For the first time since the enactment of the Voting Rights Act, Georgia's state redistricting plans were submitted for pre-clearance directly to the District of Columbia federal district court.
- For the first time, state house and congressional district plans were pre-cleared without requiring any changes.

Preliminary Maneuvering

First, Governor Barnes decided to call two special sessions: one for state legislative districts and a second for congressional districts. Never before had two separate reapportionment/redistricting special sessions been called by a governor. This action was the first clear indication that Governor Barnes planned to play a key role in the process.

Observers knew the sessions, like all previous ones, would be characterized by partisan political fireworks. Senate Republican Minority Leader Eric Johnson presaged the tone of the session two months before it convened in a guest editorial published in Georgia's leading African American GOP newspaper, the *Atlanta Daily World*, in which he wrote that drawing the districts would be about raw political power. He surmised the Democrats' strategy would be similar to past sessions where they sought to split black communities to help elect white Democrats and limit the number of black legislators who could be elected. No one predicted the major strategy that the Democrats, black and white, would ultimately adopt, which involved using Democratic voter preference data from national, statewide, and congressional elections to guide the map drawers in ensuring that Democrats could retain a majority until the 2011 redistricting session. This strategy was orchestrated primarily by Governor Barnes, but he had some allies in the General Assembly who saw it as a way to protect some Democrats from GOP challenges, as well as to prevent the loss of inner-city black Democrats as a result of GOP suburban political growth. Incumbency protection, which was the primary goal of black and white legislators, took a back seat to ensuring Democratic majorities in both houses of the legislature. It was clear from a cursory review of the demographics that focusing on single-member districts would probably ensure a Democratic majority in the house for only two to four years at most and only one session in the senate.

The redistricting process began with the traditional charge by the speaker to large county delegations to draw plans on which they could secure a consensus and submit them to the House Reapportionment Committee, which would then attempt to fit them into a statewide plan like a mosaic. During the initial phase, legislators from Atlanta (Fulton County) and Rome (Floyd County) explored the multi-member district option. The former did so in an attempt to protect a liberal Democrat who had switched from the GOP, Rep. Kathy Ashe, whose slightly GOP-leaning district was combined with a strong liberal, white, in-town neighborhood district represented by a very popular legislator, Rep. Jim

Martin, chair of the powerful House Judiciary Committee. In Rome, veteran Democrat Buddy Childs, who represented a district that included the city and fast-growing GOP suburban voters, sought to craft a two-member district to include his Democratic colleague Paul Smith, who had an overwhelmingly Democratic voting district. However, Smith opposed this effort. These two plans were the first ones submitted to the House Reapportionment Committee.

Intense negotiations between the governor and the Democratic house leadership ensued as Governor Barnes, like the "black max" proponents of the 1991 session, sought to create the maximum number of multimember districts, while the speaker and his top lieutenants favored only a minimum number. Speaker Tom Murphy was philosophically opposed to the concept of multimember districts, which had been eliminated in the 1991 redistricting because of their past use to dilute the minority vote. Initially, many GLBC members were lukewarm about multi-member districts because they remembered the "good old days" when they were used to their detriment. They were concerned that they would be sacrificed on the political altar for the benefit of white Democrats. Yet, it was clear that the almost solidly Democratic black vote in majority-black districts would have to be more evenly distributed to allow white incumbent Democrats to hold on to their seats and to create more Democratic opportunities to win elections in newly created districts. Perhaps the most significant factor in galvanizing a consensus among Democrats to adopt the multimember district strategy was a review of several proposed house single-member district plans showed that none of the plans would provide a majority of districts (91) with more than 50 percent Democratic voters. Thus, all factions of the Democratic party were united behind the desire to retain their majority.

Guidelines for Redistricting[3]

Historically, the Georgia house and senate reapportionment committees have adopted guidelines to govern their activities. A comparison of the 1991 and 2001 guidelines showed some major changes that foreshadowed the new Democratic strategy.

Public Hearings

In 1991, the joint committees decided to hold a series of public hearings in mostly urban centers throughout the state to actively seek public participation and maximize public input before and after they had adopted redistricting plans. They held 12 hearings (one meeting in each of the 10 congressional districts plus two additional meetings) throughout the state in such cities as Albany, Augusta, Columbus, Macon, Rome, Valdosta, and Savannah. In 2001, a more general statement on public hearings simply said hearings would be held without specifying any set number. In fact, only seven were held, with only two in urban areas, Atlanta and Augusta, while five were scheduled in small cities such as Brunswick, Dahlonega, Perry, Valdosta, and Watkinsville in a period of just over one month, April 17 to May 23. Even though black legislators organized busloads of African Americans to attend the public hearings, this conscious attempt to reduce the number of citizens participating in this process was successful.

Redistricting Plans

The 1991 guidelines sought to facilitate the legislature's consideration of redistricting plans and permitted individual citizens or organizations to present their plans directly to the committees. But the 2001 procedure stated that any redistricting plan presented to the committees must be sponsored by one or more members of the General Assembly. Thus, the open-ended nature of true citizen participation in the reapportionment process was closed compared to the traditional way of operating.

Single-Member vs. Multimember Districts

The 1991-1992 guidelines stated that all legislative and congressional districts "shall be single member districts." However, the 2001-2002 guidelines contained no position on this issue. Clearly, at the time these guidelines were adopted there was a decision to test the multi-member district concept after a decade of disfavor. The only question was how many such districts could be crafted that would be politically acceptable to enough Democrats to get the 91 votes needed to pass the plans.

Contiguity of Districts

One of the most glaring examples of political or racial gerrymandering was the drawing of districts that only met at adjoining corners. The 1991-1992 guidelines stated explicitly that districts should be composed of contiguous geographic areas and those that meet at points of adjoirning corners would not be deemed as contiguous. The 2001-2002 guidelines stated that the districts would be composed of contiguous geography but did not define specifically what this meant. Clearly, the lack of specificity was intentional, and districts that only met at corners were permitted. Senate Districts 16 and 24, which each stretch for more than 100 miles in length, are examples of this practice.

Criteria for Splitting Political Subdivisions

One of the most loosely defined criteria for drawing district lines concerned maintenance of communities of interest, and the many different interpretations of this term were inevitably the subject of litigation. The 1991 guidelines stated that an effort should be made to maintain the integrity of political subdivisions (precincts, cities, and counties) and the cores of existing districts and that consideration should be given to avoiding contests between incumbents. Again, the 2001-2002 language was much more general, stating only that efforts should be made to maintain the integrity of political subdivisions, i.e., not split cities or counties. There was no reference to protecting incumbency, which had been a staple of previous guidelines. Thus, Democrats attempted to place 29 GOP incumbents in single- and multi-member districts in the house, which would have effectively eliminated 15 of them; eight Republican Senators were paired in the senate.

The Governor's Role[4]

Previous Georgia governors viewed reapportionment as a legislative function and played only a minor role in the process. Prior to the administration of Lester Maddox (1967-1971), however, governors had exercised great power in the house, even effectively selecting the speaker. During the 1990s, Republicans made steady gains in both chambers and grew from a handful during the 1980s and 1990s to 24 of 56 in the senate and 74 of 180 in the house by 2000. Thus, a change of only five seats in the senate and 17 in the house would give them a majority for the first time in Georgia history.

Roy Barnes was the first Georgia governor who had to be concerned about whether he would have a working Democratic majority, which he defined as at least 36 of 56 (29 is majority) senators and 110 of 180 (91 is majority) house members. It was clear from key votes on the governor's agenda, such as changing the state flag, that there would be Democratic defections because of local and personal political considerations. While there were 105 Democrats and one Independent in the house, the demographic suburban trends pointed to significant GOP political growth for the elections of 2002 and 2004 if the legislature merely tried to protect incumbency and maintain the cores of existing districts. Obviously, this trend toward the GOP was the reason why Democrats eliminated this provision in the 2001-2002 guidelines.

The senate majority's fragility was demonstrated by several votes during the 2001-2002 legislative session. For example, on the change from the confederate symbol-dominated state flag to the new flag, only 26 Democrats voted yes. The measure would have failed without the support of six GOP senators pressured to vote yes by the Metro Atlanta Chamber of Commerce.

Thus, with the entire legislature and the governor's office up for re-election in 2002, the governor indicated that it was imperative that he ensure a Democratic majority or his legislative agenda would be in jeopardy. Indeed, the governor was the driving force and had several one-on-one sessions with reluctant legislators to get their buy-in to create a maximum number of multimember districts to encompass almost the entire state. There were intensive meetings among Democratic house members about this matter as the governor wanted to create almost twice as many multimember districts (approximately 40 with two to five seats) as the house leadership was willing to accept. The cornerstone of the strategy was to expand heavily Democratic areas into suburban GOP areas and absorb them.

House and Senate Redistricting Results[5]

In an effort to minimize the number of multimember districts, the House Reapportionment Committee drafted a working plan that included only 12 multimember districts (10 with two members each and two with three members each). The Democratic preference vote broke down as shown in the following table.

Thus, only 86 districts would have at least 50 percent Democratic preference voters, but 91 were needed for a majority. Clearly, this plan was not politically feasible.

Districts With a Majority of Democratic Preference Voters in Multimember District Plan

Democratic Preference Voters (%)	Number of Members	Number of Districts
54	64	62
52–53.99	18	15
50–51.99	9	9

Two days after the first special session began on August 14, 2001, the House Reapportionment Committee adopted a plan with 12 multimember districts, some with two representatives and some with three. The plan created 91 districts with 50 percent or more Democratic-preference voters and 10 districts with between 48 and 49.99 percent Democratic-preference voters. Speaker Murphy was in a two-member district that was designed to bolster his Democratic-preference percentage. He had won the general election in 2000 by less than 200 votes.

House GOP leaders criticized the plan as did some Democratic members. Minority Leader Lynn Westmoreland said the plan was an attempt to reduce the number of Republican legislators by 25 and promised that the GOP would win the 17 seats needed to become the majority party in the house. He also expressed resentment at Governor Barnes' attempt to dictate redistricting and asserted that the electorate would resent his meddling and vote for the candidate, not the party. Actually, the house leadership had negotiated the plan with the governor after several members had expressed reservations about running in multimember districts.

On August 15, 2001, the house passed House Bill 1EX1 by a vote of 102 to 74 after four GOP amendments were defeated on party-line votes. As the speaker was announcing the results, the 74 Republican house members began walking out of the chambers. Following precedent, the senate passed the house plan without any amendments. However, in another first, Governor Barnes vetoed the bill, citing minority vote dilution in two districts.

The first special session ended without an approved house redistricting plan. During the second session called to address congressional redistricting, the house committee "cleaned up" or "tweaked" the plan in HB 1EX2, which reduced the number of multimember districts from 24 to 23 and created two additional majority-black districts. The new plan contained two districts with four seats, six with three seats, and 14 with two seats. The revised plan passed both houses on party-line votes.

Governor Barnes basically dictated the senate district plan. As indicated, there was little room for defection in the senate, with its slim 32-member Democratic majority and 29 votes required to enact legislation. As expected, the senate GOP leader criticized the governor for meddling in the General Assembly's area of responsibility. The initial proposal paired six GOP senators in three districts, moved four other Republicans into heavily Democratic voting districts with strong Democratic incumbents, and created seven new competitive districts. The goal was for Democrats to gain two to seven new seats. However, some Democratic senators (four black and one white) objected to the configuration of their districts. Consequently, the senate plan was withdrawn, reworked, and resubmitted to the full senate three days later.

Ralph Reed, former head of the Christian Coalition and recently elected chair of the Georgia GOP, said the plan was unconstitutional and would not survive a court suit. Referring to the reduction of several majority-black districts below 60 percent BVAP, Reed called it a step backwards for minority representation. The governor believed the reductions were critical for white Democrats to win elections in adjacent districts. African American Senator David Scott, chair of the Senate Rules Committee, said the plan conformed to the VRA and would help elect more black senators. Senate Minority Leader Eric Johnson predicted Governor Barnes would experience a political backlash from the Georgia electorate for drawing such gerrymandered districts to give Democrats an advantage in the 2002 general election.

When Senate Bill 1EX1 reached the floor on August 10, eighteen GOP senators began to filibuster; three actually cried when they talked about the strangely shaped districts. Reed held another press conference and asserted the federal courts would declare the plan unconstitutional because it diluted minority voting strength and destroyed local communities of interest. Lieutenant Governor Mark Taylor said it was a great day in Georgia, and black Majority Leader Charles Walker said Senator Johnson's concern about black voters being used as pawns was patronizing and commented that the GOP's voting record over the years showed their true feelings toward minorities in Georgia—Republicans had never been supportive of their interests. The senate plan passed by a vote of 29 to 26.

Congressional Redistricting Outcomes[6]

Congressional redistricting proved to be very divisive for Democrats. The speaker was determined that Bob Barr would not continue to represent his district in Congress. Four black senators threatened to vote against all plans created by a conference committee without a black representative from the Atlanta region. Without their support, Democrats were one short of the number needed for adoption of a plan. Eighteen members of the house GLBC formed a coalition that passed a substitute plan, rather than the one proposed by the speaker. The alternative plan, drawn by their Black Augusta colleague, Representative Ben Allen, would provide him with an opportunity to be elected in the new Twelfth Congressional District.

The senate was deadlocked on the congressional plan. The governor had directed his three floor leaders to oppose the reapportionment committee plan. Four black Atlanta senators "locked down" against any plan with less than a 38 percent BVAP in the newly created metro Atlanta district, and Senator Dan Lee of LaGrange objected to the plan because of local political reasons. Thus, at most there were only 25 of the 29 votes needed to pass a plan out of the senate. Similarly in the house, 18 of the 36 members of the GLBC informed the speaker they would vote against his committee plan in the full house and for the Allen substitute, but he ignored them and suffered defeat as a coalition of blacks, Republicans, and dissident white Democrats passed the Allen plan. The senate passed an amended plan, objected to the house plan, then passed the Allen plan, and a conference committee was formed.

Four African American senators from the Atlanta area were adamant about creating two congressional districts—one in the Atlanta area and another in the Augusta area—with close to a 40 percent BVAP. The governor was interested in a district for David Worley, his chosen chair of the state Democratic party, and former opponent of Newt Gingrich (he lost by less than 500 votes). Clayton County Senator Greg Hecht was a favorite of the Senate Pro Tem Terrell Starr. Other agendas included transforming the delegation from eight white Republicans and three black Democrats to seven Democrats and six Republicans; avoiding a plan that would provoke one of the popular GOP Congressmen, such as Saxby Chambliss, Mack Collins, or Jack Kingston, to run against Democratic incumbent Senator Max Cleland or Governor Barnes in the November 2002 election; and blocking Bob Barr from representing Harrelson County, the speaker's home county.

The senate took the lead in drawing the congressional map and unveiled SB 1EX2 on August 28, 2001. The new Thirteenth District had a 46 percent minority population (36.12 percent black and 9.95 percent Hispanic), and the Twelfth District was also 46 percent minority (43.21 percent black and 2.9 percent Hispanic). Seven districts, including those of the three black Democratic incumbents, had a majority of Democratic-preference voters. Governor Barnes objected to his home county of Cobb being split among four congressional districts.

As the various conflicting agendas collided, the Democratic leadership became factionalized. Negotiations were so intense that a four-day recess was taken. Three black members were on the conference committee, including two from the senate, but the black senior senator David Scott was adamant that Atlanta had to have one of the three senate conferees or he and his three colleagues would not support any plan. Black Senate Majority Leader Charles Walker of Augusta was replaced by Atlanta-Dekalb Senator Nadine Thomas. A compromise plan seemed imminent as Lieutenant Governor Taylor got his three south Georgia districts, and black legislators had their two new districts with 38 percent BVAP. However, the governor was still disturbed over the split of Cobb County among four congressional districts, and he instructed his senate floor leader and two assistant floor leaders to oppose the plan. And since Senator Lee was also still in opposition, the senate Democrats were one short of a majority. In a pique of frustration, Lieutenant Governor Taylor at 10 p.m. tried to adjourn the senate and end the special session without a congressional plan, as had occurred in 1995. The governor also urged the house leadership to pass an adjournment resolution, but his effort failed. The speaker convened the house committee chairs to consider adjournment, and they agreed to oppose the senate resolution, voting against the resolution to adjourn at 11:30 p.m. by a margin of 2 to 1.

The GOP argued that the General Assembly should go home and reconvene later in the fall or in January during the regular session to draw a congressional map. The house decided to recess for four days and reconvene on September 26 to give the Democrats a chance to "cool off" and then try to work out an agreement. Little progress had been made when the legislature reconvened, and the GOP again called for adjournment. The Democrats were persistent, but the house and senate both passed resolutions to adjourn at midnight on Friday, September 28. The senate had inexplicably decided to return to the capitol on Friday, September 28, rather than Wednesday, September 26. The conferees continued their negotiations. Finally, on Friday afternoon of the 28th, the six conferees agreed on a map; however, it was five hours later at about 8 p.m. before the plan was ready for presentation and a vote.

Just before the conference report had lain on the desk for one hour as required by house rules, some noncontroversial resolutions were passed with only 137 members voting. Recognizing that a large number of Democrats were off the floor, House Minority Leader Lynn Westmoreland attempted a parliamentary maneuver to stop debate and force a vote on the conference committee report when it came up. The Democrats, who were scattered around the building, quickly returned to the house chambers to thwart the maneuver. After brief appeals from the conferees to adopt the report and Westmoreland's speech urging opposition, the house voted 99 to 59 and the senate 30 to 23 to adopt the committee report. Thus did the General Assembly temporarily end the politics of reapportionment.

2001-2002 Redistricting—Role of the Black Caucus and Effects on Black Representation

In all previous redistricting sessions, black Democrats had little influence in the legislature's redrawing of the district lines, except for a small number of districts within urban counties. Traditionally, the state was divided into regions, and legislators in each body would determine the districts within their area, which would then be fitted into a statewide plan after some tweaking. African American legislators played a minor role, and their influence was mostly exerted through the DOJ, which usually rejected the state-drawn plans and forced the legislature to redraw their proposed maps to maximize the potential for black representation.

This tactic worked until the mid-1990s, when the U.S. Supreme Court developed a new doctrine of reverse discrimination in *Miller v. Johnson*, which said race could not be used as the primary criterion in drawing legislative district boundaries. After the court's 1995 decision, the white Democrats used the special reapportionment session to eliminate nine majority-black state house districts and two senate districts held by powerful white legislators. Incredibly, a majority of black Democrats voted for these new maps. In 2001, the GLBC showed great flexibility in pursing their goals and black incumbents agreed to reduce the BVAP percentages in their districts and also to run in multimember districts. For them, it was a win-win situation since they wanted Democrats to retain a majority in the legislature, keep their chairs of committees, and regain control of the state's congressional delegation.

In the special session held in 1995, the house and senate could not reach a consensus on a congressional plan, and a south Georgia federal district court drew the new congressional districts. Only one of the three majority-black congressional districts survived, while the other two were reduced from 62 to 36 percent BVAP and from 54 to 35 percent BVAP.

In 2001, black senators led by David Scott from Atlanta effectively blocked the senate from drawing the boundaries of the new congressional districts (Twelfth and Thirteenth) until the demographics were changed to increase black populations to 38 percent each and total minority population to 46 percent, to enhance the electoral prospects of African American candidates for these two seats. Although the lieutenant governor's three nominees to the Reapportionment Conference Committee included two African Americans, Scott and his three Senate colleagues held fast until an Atlanta area legislator was appointed. The speaker also appointed a black member to the conference committee. In the 1990s, there was one black on the congressional conference committee, but in 2001 three of the six members were black.

The GLBC also had a major role in state legislative redistricting. It played an integral role in determining the number and size of multimember districts as well as the minimum black population percentage and Democratic preference vote. Consequently, the GLBC was expected to add four to seven black state representatives. In the senate, one black member, Senator Regina Thomas, objected to the black population reduction in her district. The federal district court agreed in April 2002 and required an increase in the black percentage in not only her district but two others as well. It was anticipated that two additional African American senators would be elected in 2002. Overall, the GLBC had its most successful redistricting session in the history of the legislature.

Separate Agendas

The Democrats were unified in desiring to retain a majority, but differed on the strategy to achieve that goal. The governor sought to ensure as many multimember districts with a majority of Democratic preference voters as possible. The speaker gave greater weight to incumbency protection and single-member districts. Black legislators sought to increase their state legislative numbers and draw lines to provide a chance for blacks to win in two new congressional seats. The resulting compromise plans gave each major player partial victories.

Concerning the state legislative plans, the speaker and his top lieutenants wanted to protect white Democratic incumbents and favored a single-member district plan. They subsequently negotiated a compromise with the governor to reduce the number of multimember districts and draw lines to protect allies.

Governor Barnes was focused on creating the maximum number of multimember and Democratic preference congressional and state legislative districts regardless of whether Democratic incumbents were protected. Also, he wanted to protect his home county of Cobb from being split among four congressional districts. His goal was to ensure a working Democratic majority for the entire first decade of the twenty-first century so Democrats would be in a position to control the redistricting process in 2011. The GLBC concentrated on gaining more majority-black state and congressional districts. Jim Wooten, associate editor of the *Atlanta Constitution*, asserted that while white and black Democratic legislators were united in trying to preserve their monopoly of political power, they differed over how to distribute the black voters. He concluded that all three Democratic factions seemed prepared to sacrifice black rural voters to guarantee that white Democrats would be elected by making their districts 30 to 40 percent black.

Democratic Performance: The Primary Criterion

The concept of Democratic preference dominated the session. The governor used election results in the 1996, 1998, and 2000 elections to ascertain the Democratic preference vote. Statewide races involving black candidates were examined as well as the presidential election of 2000.

The final house plan, which contained 23 multimember districts with 56 representatives, was a result of tough negotiations. A total of 102 districts with more than 50 percent Democratic preference voters were included in the plan (66 at 54.91 percent; 28 at 52-53.99 percent, and 8 at 50-51.99 percent). The senate plan was basically the governor's plan, which had 36 districts with more than 50 percent Democratic preference voters. BVAP was also considered in an attempt to avoid retrogression in some districts. There was some criticism of using statewide and national election results to ascertain the Democratic preference vote. Some thought local and state legislative races should have been incorporated in the analysis since voting patterns sometimes vary based on the level of the election. This issue was debated in the District of Columbia federal district court case in which the court on April 9, 2002, approved the congressional and house plans, but required changes in three senate districts to prevent retrogression.

When the House Reapportionment Committee drafted a single-member district plan to provide for a Democratic majority, the numbers simply did not work. Only 79 districts would have a Democratic majority, as follows:

52 districts	54+ percent Democratic preference
19 districts	52-53.99 percent Democratic preference
8 districts	50-51.99 percent Democratic preference

Multimember Districts

Multimember districts became the cornerstone of the governor's strategy, which permitted expansion of heavily Democratic areas into suburban GOP areas to absorb them. The governor's original plan would have created about 40 such districts, ranging from two to five seats each. However, the house leaders would not agree to this proposal. They and the full house voted for a 23 multimember district plan with 56 of 180 members in multimember districts. The speaker, who initially was in a two-member district, changed his mind and returned to a single-member district, which actually reduced the Democratic preference percentage in his district. A total of 29 Republican house members were paired in the same districts, five were placed in majority-Democratic single-member districts, and one was put in a district held by a popular Independent incumbent. In the senate, eight Republicans were paired in four districts and four others were placed in heavily Democratic districts with incumbents. Four of the GOP congressmen were paired in two congressional districts.

End of the Black-GOP Alliance

In previous redistricting, black interests in creating more majority seats coincided with GOP interests. During the 2001 session, there was no speculation about a tacit black-Republican alliance, even though the senate and house minority leaders talked about how black legislators were being sacrificed in both bodies in order for the white Democratic leadership to retain power.

Submission of Plans to Federal Court for Preclearance

Finally, to expedite action and secure a final determination of whether the three plans would get federal approval, for the first time in history all were sent directly to the federal district court in Washington, DC, rather than to the DOJ for preclearance. The court approved the congressional and house plans, but required changes in three senate districts to increase the black voting-age population. These changes were completed on April 9, 2002, by the General Assembly during the lengthy regular session. The court increased Senate

District 2 (Savannah) up to 53.6 percent black, Senate District 26 (Macon) to 54 percent, and Senate District 12 (Albany) to 55 percent. However, it permitted an elongated Republican-dominated District 24 to stretch almost 130 miles from near Augusta to Spalding County in metro Atlanta.

Mixed Results in November 2002 and Prospects for the Future

The effects of the Democratic-controlled redistricting process on minority representation were mixed, based on the November 5, 2002, elections for state legislative and congressional seats. One major breakthrough, however, was the willingness of black legislators to trade off lower black percentages in exchange for maintaining Democratic majorities in the General Assembly. Black legislators were even willing to accept the multimember district concept. In return, they asserted themselves forcefully into the congressional redistricting process and forced the white Democratic leadership to adhere to their demands to draw Georgia's two new districts with a 46 percent minority voting-age population, and they even succeeded in getting three of the six members on the conference committee that drew the final maps. With growing seniority, the recent retirement of senior white Democrats, and the likelihood of retaining a Democratic majority in the legislature, the prospects were good for increasing the number of African Americans in leadership positions and black political influence in the General Assembly after the 2002 election.

Five additional black legislators were elected in the house, thus raising their numbers from 34 to 39. There was, however, a net loss of one in the senate, as local political issues resulted in the defeat of Senate Majority Leader Charles Walker as well as the defeat of three African American candidates by Hispanic candidate Sam Zammarippa for the seat vacated by Senator Scott, who was elected to the new 13th Congressional District seat. Senator Walker's son, Charles "Champ" Walker, Jr., won the Democratic nomination for a U.S. House seat (District 12), but he lost in the general election as a result of several major political campaign mistakes and political opposition to his father by black ministers and white civic and political leaders. All of the white congressional incumbents retained their seats as did black incumbents John Lewis and Sanford Bishop, but Cynthia McKinney was defeated in the Democratic primary by Denise Majette, an African American state court judge from Dekalb County, who also won the November general election.

Only one white Democratic candidate, Jim Marshall, former mayor of Macon, was elected to bring the total number of Democrats in the congressional delegation to five. Finally, Democrats were able to increase their numbers to 107 in the state house with 72 Republicans and one Independent; while in the state senate their margin was reduced by 2 to give them a 30-to-26 majority. Governor Barnes, who spent $19 million in his re-election campaign, was upset by GOP candidate Sonny Perdue, who spent only $3 million. Political analysts attributed Barnes' loss to his alienation of several influential groups, including teachers and opponents of both the state flag change and the controversial Northern Arc Expressway.

Two startling developments occurred shortly after the November election. Four Democratic Senators switched parties to give the GOP a 30 to 26 majority. And Tom Murphy, the longest-serving speaker in the nation, lost his re-election bid. In the contest to succeed him, Representative Terry Coleman, chair of Appropriations, won the Democratic nomination for speaker, defeating former Democratic Majority Leader Larry Walker, who had attempted to ally with Governor-Elect Perdue to form a coalition with the House GOP members against Coleman. The vote was 109-70.

The battle is not over yet. Despite the court decisions in the 1990s, all black congressional and state legislative incumbents won re-election in redrawn majority-white districts. Also, the federal district court in Washington, DC, has developed a new legal precedent that defines retrogression as the impact of an entire plan rather than that of individual districts.

The success of the GLBC in the 2001 reapportionment process demonstrated increasing political influence in the General Assembly. However, political observers will be watching the 2003-2004 legislative session closely to see if GOP gains will prevent GLBC members from passing legislation beneficial to their constituencies.

NOTES

1 For detailed information on reapportionment/redistricting in these years, see "The 1991 Special Session," in *The Georgia Legislative Review 1991*, edited by Bob Holmes and Gretchen E. MacLachan (Atlanta, GA: Southern Center for Studies in Public Policy [SCSPP]), 1991), 92-106; and Bob Holmes, "Reapportionment and Redistricting" in *The Georgia Legislative Review 1992*, edited by Bob Holmes and Gretchen E. MacLachan (Atlanta: SCSPP, 1992), 109-123.

2 This section is based on Bob Holmes, "The Redistricting/Reapportionment Special Session," in *The Georgia Legislative Review 1995*, edited by Bob Holmes and Gretchen E. MacLachan (Atlanta, GA: SCSPP, 1995), 145-163.

3 This section is based on two mimeographed documents distributed by the House Reapportionment Committee, "Guidelines Adopted by the House Committee on Congressional and Legislative Reapportionment and Redistricting 1991-1992" and "2001-2002 Guidelines for the House Senate Committee on Congressional and Legislative Reapportionment and Redistricting."

4 The analysis in this section and other references to Governor Barnes' activities are based on an interview with Barnes by the author, May 3, 2002.

5 The discussion of the General Assembly activities related to redistricting/reapportionment during the 2001 legislative session is based on Bob Holmes, "Epilogue: The Special Session on Reapportionment/Redistricting" in *The Georgia Legislative Review 2001*, edited by Bob Holmes (Atlanta, GA: SCSPP, 2001), 127-135.

6 Much of the discussion of the political maneuvering and strategies and tactics concerning the role of major political players in the reapportionment drama is based on a review of numerous maps and data, plus an interview with Linda Meggers, head of General Reapportionment Staff, Georgia General Assembly, May 1, 2002.

7. Racial Redistricting and Southern Republican Congressional Gains in the 1990s

David Lublin

Despite sporadic efforts by Democrats to limit the damage to their party, racial redistricting has systematically aided the election of Republican congressional and state legislative candidates in the South.

A product of the Voting Rights Act, as interpreted by the courts, racial redistricting is the creation of majority-minority districts for the purpose of making possible the election of candidates preferred by the minority community, often called "candidates of choice." Section 5 of the act requires covered jurisdictions to submit their redistricting plans to the U.S. attorney general for preclearance.[1] If the attorney general is convinced that a plan reduces the influence of minority votes, he can object to the plan and prevent it from going into effect. The original 1965 version of the act designated Alabama, Georgia, Louisiana, Mississippi, South Carolina, Virginia, and portions of North Carolina as covered jurisdictions. During renewals of the act, Congress added a number of other jurisdictions, including places outside the South. Section 2 of the Voting Rights Act allows plaintiffs to file suit on the basis of alleged minority vote dilution, even if the attorney general does not object to the plan under Section 5.

The U.S. Supreme Court created a three-pronged test for vote dilution in a 1986 decision, *Thornburg v. Gingles.* According to the *Gingles* test, Section 2 of the Voting Rights Act compels courts to order the creation of new majority-minority districts if a minority group is:

(1) Sufficiently large and geographically compact to constitute a majority in a single member district,

(2) Politically cohesive, and

(3) Usually unable to elect its preferred candidate due to racial bloc voting.

The first condition requires that there must be a viable solution to the problem of vote dilution for a court to act. Without overturning the electoral system, courts cannot address the problem of vote dilution if it is not possible to draw a majority-minority district. More recent U.S. Supreme Court decisions, such as *Shaw v. Reno* and *Miller v. Johnson*, have effectively given more weight to this concept of geographic compactness. These decisions have effectively limited the ability of states to create majority-minority districts with particularly odd shapes or boundaries.

The next prong of the *Gingles* test requires that members of the minority group consistently vote as a bloc. It makes little sense to create new majority-minority districts to advance minority interests if minority members cannot agree on those interests or on a political party to advance them. Demonstrating political cohesion has usually been relatively easy for plaintiffs because of strong support by African Americans for the Democratic Party. Of course, cohesion is not the same as unanimity. Individual African Americans may vote for GOP candidates, even as the overwhelming share of black voters regularly cast their ballots for Democratic candidates.

The last prong of the *Gingles* test is crucial. Plaintiffs must show that racial bloc voting is so severe that the minority consistently cannot elect its preferred candidate. To win a case under the *Gingles* test, plaintiffs must prove that the cohesiveness of the white majority allows it to regularly defeat the black minority. Providing evidence that most whites vote for one candidate and most blacks another is not enough to prove racial bloc voting under the *Gingles* test. After all, the black-preferred candidate can still win election with a coalition of united black support and a minority of white voters. According to *Gingles*, it is unnecessary for a court to act if the black-preferred candidate can win.

African Americans have almost always selected African American candidates when given the opportunity to choose between them and non-black candidates. But many African American candidates have not been able to amass enough white support to win outside a majority-black district. As a result, plaintiffs in voting rights cases have often found it a straightforward matter to satisfy the last prong of the *Gingles* test. Generally, white candidates have had better luck in majority-black districts.

All but one of the new majority-black congressional districts created during the 1990s redistricting round were in the South. Alabama, Louisiana, South Carolina, Texas, and Virginia each drew one new majority-black congressional district. At the same time, Georgia and North Carolina each drew two new majority-black districts. African Americans experienced the largest gains in Florida as the Sunshine State added three new majority-black districts. During its renewal in 1975, the Voting Rights Act's reach was extended to apply to language minorities, including Latinos. New majority-Latino districts were created in both Florida and Texas prior to the 1992 elections for the U.S. House of Representatives.

Legal Battles

With the greatly increased number of majority-minority districts following the 1990s round of redistricting, racial redistricting has come under intense legal scrutiny. Starting with its decision in *Shaw v. Reno*, the Supreme Court articulated a new theory, according to which making race the "predominant factor" in redistricting violates the Fourteenth Amendment's Equal Protection Clause. In an opinion for the Court, Justice Sandra Day O'Connor stated her belief that placing blacks and whites into different districts perpetuates racial stereotypes of blacks and whites as political opponents. The Court's swing justice further contended that racial redistricting could "balkanize" America and "bears an uncomfortable resemblance to political apartheid."[2]

Unfortunately, election returns strongly indicate that blacks and whites usually do vote quite differently and that these electoral patterns make it hard for many blacks to win election from majority-white districts. Rather than being "balkanized," many black-majority districts are among the most racially mixed in the country. Blacks composed only 53 percent of the voting-age population in the much-attacked North Carolina Twelfth District. A bare majority does not suggest the racially pure districts implied by references to apartheid. Even if blacks out-vote whites in majority-black districts, the result is exactly parallel to that encountered by blacks in most congressional districts. In contrast to its attack on racial redistricting, the Supreme Court has permitted districts with bizarre boundaries when drawn for partisan purposes. It is therefore not shocking that civil rights advocates may conclude that the Court's demands for compactness for majority-minority districts place a discriminatory burden on minority plaintiffs.

Prominent scholars, including Abigail Thernstrom and Carol Swain, have argued that African Americans can win election without racial redistricting. Unfortunately, both Thernstrom and Swain depend largely on anecdotal evidence to prove their case.[3] The preponderance of scholarly evidence from more systematic studies of the question indicates that African American and Latino candidates usually find it difficult to win election in majority-white districts.[4] However, more recent studies by some of these same scholars provide some evidence that African Americans can secure the Democratic nomination and then win the general election in selected majority-white districts.[5]

The Negative Impact of Racial Redistricting on Democracts

The most telling criticism of racial redistricting may be that it undermines the representation of minority interests even as it assures the election of more racial minorities to the U.S. House of Representatives. The outcome seems illogical at first, especially since these same studies conclude that African American representatives are especially likely to be responsive to the concerns of African American voters. The problem does not stem from the actions of minority representatives, but from the impact of the creation of new majority-minority districts on elections in neighboring districts. Placing black Democrats into majority-black districts requires cutting their numbers in neighboring districts. As a result, these adjoining districts become more likely to elect a Republican instead of a Democrat. Creating one new district for a black Democrat may require sacrificing a white Democrat. Since white Democrats lend greater support than do Republicans to initiatives advocated by African Americans, racial redistricting has the potential to undercut overall levels of legislative support for policies supported by blacks.

Imagining the impact of racial redistricting on two hypothetical 40-percent-black districts may help to explain this seemingly paradoxical outcome of racial redistricting. If redistricting alters the boundaries between the two districts in order to make one of the two districts 65 percent black, the other district must inevitably have fewer black voters and become only 15 percent black. African American candidates almost never fail to win election from 65 percent black districts.[6] The election of a new black representative is all but guaranteed from the new majority-black district. On the other hand, the probability of its neighbor electing a Republican representative will rise considerably. Republicans only rarely win in 35 percent black districts because winning in such districts requires that they receive a very high, indeed difficult-to-obtain share of the white vote. However, Republican candidates regularly win election from 15 percent black districts. The probability of a Republican winning election tends to increase as the white share of the district's population rises.[7]

The actual impact of racial redistricting on the outcome of Georgia congressional contests vividly shows the potential downside of racial redistricting for Democrats. During the 1990 redistricting, Georgia was forced by the U.S. Justice Department to create two new majority-black districts.[8] Rep. John Lewis had represented the sole previously existing majority-black district in the U.S. House since 1986. African American Democrats carried all three majority-black districts in the 1992 election. Lewis easily won reelection from his Atlanta-based district, and the two new majority-black districts were won by Sanford Bishop and Cynthia McKinney. Bishop defeated a white incumbent in the Democratic primary in a district centered on southwestern Georgia. McKinney won election from a district nicknamed the "Sherman's March District" because it swept across the state from Savannah to Atlanta.

As a result of creating two new majority-black districts, the black share of the population declined in several other Georgia districts, with unhappy consequences for white Democratic candidates. Incumbent Democrat Richard Ray lost his re-election battle after redistricting cut the black share of his district's population by 16 percent. Republican Jack Kingston won an open seat after redistricting sliced its black population by 10 percent. Republican John Linder very narrowly won another open seat in which redistricting had reduced its black population by just over 1 percent, more than his margin of victory.[9]

Limiting the Damage

In some states, Democrats were able to counter the negative impact of racial redistricting on their party through partisan gerrymandering. Democrats adopted congressional district plans in Louisiana, North Carolina, Texas, and Virginia that included new majority-minority districts but also were carefully crafted to prevent Republicans from making gains as a result. Packing Republicans was a key part of all of these plans, since concentrating Republicans in certain districts hurts the GOP just as concentrating African Americans in majority-black districts hurts Democrats. At the same time, Democrats tried not to put more minorities in majority-minority districts than were absolutely necessary for minorities to win election and to avoid a lawsuit or Section 5 objection by the Justice Department. This approach allowed the Democrats to place some minority Democrats in other districts in order to shore up the political bases of white Democrats. Democratic gerrymanders thus attempted to limit the damage that racial redistricting posed to the overall fortunes of the party.

However, Democratic mapmakers had to draw noncompact districts with bizarre boundaries in order to accommodate both their partisan and racial goals. These plans invariably violated more county boundaries than earlier plans. North Carolina arguably adopted the most extreme plan as its congressional map contained four districts contiguous only at a single point. By meeting at a single point, the plan allowed one district to leap over another yet adhere to the requirement for contiguous congressional districts.

Of course, even the most carefully calibrated partisan gerrymander may not succeed in protecting Democrats. In 1994, the Republicans picked up four seats in North Carolina despite the artful map adopted by the Democrats. The Democrats had mistakenly assumed that their party's vote share would remain unchanged. However, the Democratic plan was highly vulnerable to any decline in the overall Democratic share of the vote. Racial redistricting removed the cushion provided by black Democrats against a swing to the GOP among white voters. African American Democrats are more loyal to their party than are white Democrats, so any swing against the Democrats would likely occur among white voters. As white Democratic voters now had greater numbers, pro-Republican shifts in voting behavior were more likely to hurt them than in the past. When many whites did abandon the Democrats in the 1994 mid-term elections, the impact was exacerbated by racial redistricting.

Moreover, starting with *Shaw v. Reno* in 1993, the Supreme Court severely undercut efforts by Democrats to enact partisan gerrymanders intended to limit the harm to the party caused by racial redistricting. Declaring that the new majority-minority districts with odd and erratic borders were "racial gerrymanders," the Supreme Court compelled states to either eliminate majority-minority districts or make the districts more compact. The latter solution was especially devastating to Democratic efforts to draw new majority-minority seats and protect other seats held by white Democrats. All of the Democratic congressional gerrymanders were eventually struck down by the courts as racial gerrymanders. Over the long term, the Court's decision may actually aid Democratic efforts to win more House seats because there will be fewer packed Democratic districts. However, the incumbency advantage has allowed many Republican incumbents to continue to win seats over the short term even after new districting plans added more African American Democrats to their districts.

Even if the Supreme Court had not struck down some of the most creative gerrymanders, racial redistricting would still likely harm Democrats. Democrats either lacked the power to enact partisan gerrymanders in most states with new majority-minority districts or chose not to do so. For example, the new majority-black congressional district created in Alabama as part of a court-drawn plan probably lost the Democrats two seats to the Republicans.[10] In Georgia, Democrats in the state legislature were so intent on ending Republican Newt Gingrich's career that they failed to notice that their plan endangered several white Democrats.[11]

Estimated Democratic Losses in Congress and State Legislatures

The number of seats that racial redistricting cost the Democrats in both congressional and state legislative elections is presented in Table 7.1. Due to racial redistricting, Democrats lost an estimated ten seats in four states: Alabama, Florida, Georgia, and North Carolina. However, Democrats in Virginia adopted a particularly successful plan and managed to gain one seat through racial redistricting. Except for racial redistricting, the GOP majority in the U.S. House of Representatives would have been around one-third smaller in 1995. The GOP might have experienced even greater gains at the expense of the Democrats due to racial redistricting if the Democrats had not adopted pro-Democratic congressional maps in four other states.

Democrats found it harder to protect their partisans from redistricting losses in the 2000 redistricting round. Crafting partisan gerrymanders usually requires control of the governor's office and both houses of the state legislature. Republican growth over the course of the 1990s gave the GOP control of a number of southern states and weakened Democratic control of others. In other states, Republican governors were able to block plans passed by Democratic legislatures. *Shaw v. Reno* and its progeny limited the packing of black and Latino Democrats into new majority-minority districts. This probably will prevent further losses due to racial redistricting after the 2000 redistricting round. Some states, however, responded to the judicial attack on racial redistricting by altering their plans just enough to satisfy the courts while preserving the racial and partisan status quo.[12] Combined with the incumbency advantage held by entrenched Republican incumbents, plans constructed to minimize change could make it difficult for Democrats to recover previous redistricting losses.

Table 7.1 further presents redistricting losses for southern state houses. The table also divides these losses into those caused by the independent effect of racial redistricting and those due to the interaction between racial redistricting and a vote swing to the Republicans. Losses caused by the independent effect of racial redistricting are losses that occurred only because of changes in the boundaries of the district. Even if they won the same vote share, the Democrats would have lost these seats because of the alteration in the aggregation of votes into districts. Interaction losses are those resulting from shifts in district lines and vote swings to the GOP. These losses are not losses due only to gains in the Republican vote share. Losses resulting from a hemorrhage in the Democratic vote are counted under vote swing losses. In contrast, interaction losses are losses that would not have taken place but for the combination of the changes in district boundaries and the gain in Republican votes.

Other observers might label these interaction losses as the unexpected impact of racial redistricting, as the Democrats hardly thought that the GOP would make such large vote gains. In short, they might assert that these losses were caused by the rise in the Republican vote share.[13] However, these Republican gains were really due to redistricting because the vote swing would have taken place regardless of whether new majority-minority districts were drawn. If African Americans had not been concentrated into new black majority districts, the Democrats would not have lost the seats.

The Democrats also experienced losses due to racial redistricting at the state legislative level. Racial redistricting explains 45 of the 105 seats that slipped out of Democratic hands in the 1990 to 1994 period. The 45 seats are equal to 3.7 percent of all of the state house seats in the region. Even if one only includes districts lost because of the independent effect of redistricting, racial redistricting explains about one-third of Republican gains over this period.

The Democrats paid an especially high price due to racial redistricting in Florida, Georgia, and South Carolina, where redistricting cost the Democrats 7.6, 5.5, and 6.7 percent, respectively, of state house districts. In South Carolina, the Democrats would still hold a majority in the state house if racial redistricting had not originally cost them control in 1992. In a similar vein, the North Carolina GOP would have lost control back to the Democrats two years earlier in 1996 if racial redistricting had not made it harder for the Democrats to gain back the necessary seats. But for racial redistricting, Democrats also would have kept control of the Virginia house instead of having to share control with the Republicans in 1998.[14]

One must be careful to note that racial redistricting was clearly not the principal cause of Democratic losses to the Republicans. The movement of white southern voters to the Republicans was the cause of most state legislative losses. And losses that occurred in the latter part of the 1990s were usually not due to racial redistricting. Moreover, racial redistricting was hardly fatal to the Democratic Party in many states. Despite the creation of new majority-minority districts, the Democrats managed to recapture the North Carolina state house in 1998 and retain it in the 2000 elections. Incredibly enough, in Mississippi, Democrats gained seats in the 1999 elections even though they already occupied over two-thirds of state house districts prior to the election.

Impact on Elite Incentives and Opportunities

The creation of new majority-minority districts changes the political context by eliminating majority-white districts with sizeable shares of minority voters. Instead, states draw more majority-minority districts and more heavily white seats. White Democrats find it harder to win election from either majority-minority districts or heavily white districts than from districts with a white majority and a substantial minority presence. As shown in Table 7.2, reducing the number of African Americans in a state legislative district tends to make Democrats more vulnerable to defeat by a Republican in the general election. Similarly, white Democrats find it harder to win election over a minority opponent in majority-minority districts.[15] Since racial redistricting reduces the number of districts amenable to white Democratic candidates, it provides white politicians with a strong incentive to seek office under the GOP banner.

Table 7.3 reveals that the impact of racial redistricting on the distribution of districts by racial composition was substantial in both state legislative and congressional elections. Racial redistricting eliminated many seats in districts that are greater than 20 percent but less than 50 percent black, the seats most likely to elect white Democrats. Due to racial redistricting, the share of majority-black districts grew in every state. As a direct consequence of racial redistricting, the portion of districts that are less than 20 black also rose. With these changes, the political environment became much less friendly to white

Democrats even as new opportunities were provided for both white Republicans and black Democrats.

Racial redistricting thus sped up the polarization of southern politics by reducing the number of moderate white Democrats in favor of more liberal minority Democrats and more conservative white Republicans. It also restructured the state legislative and congressional districts in a way that limits opportunities for white Democrats and expands them for white Republicans. The growing strength of the Republicans within legislative chambers only adds to their appeal as the GOP actually holds power or appears a serious contender for it in many more chambers than before 1992. Ultimately, Democrats may suffer less from the short-term problem of loss of seats in the U.S. House and state legislatures and more from the long-term impact on the choices made by aspiring white politicians. Politicians pay close attention to the political context when selecting a course of action.

Racial Redistricting in the New Century

If the 1990s was a decade of upheaval from the perspective of both redistricting and political change, the first decade of the new century promises to be a bit quieter. The year 1992 saw the creation of numerous new majority-black districts throughout the South and new majority-Latino districts in Florida and Texas. Although the number of elected African American and Latino Democrats increased dramatically due to this policy, the total number of Democrats declined. Packing black Democrats into majority-minority districts proved detrimental to the party preferred by most African Americans.

The judicial reaction against racial redistricting resulted in the redrawing of congressional districts with minority incumbents in six southern states. Courts forced Florida, Georgia, Louisiana, North Carolina, Texas, and Virginia to adjust their congressional district boundaries or simply undertook the task themselves. Additionally, as part of a legal settlement of a racial gerrymandering lawsuit, South Carolina agreed to do the same during the 2000 redistricting round.

Several minority incumbents found themselves in majority-white districts after the process of retrenchment was complete. However, only Louisiana Rep. Cleo Fields, who saw his district virtually abolished from under him, declined to seek re-election. All other African American and Latino incumbents sought and won re-election in their reconfigured districts. Even if minorities did not form a majority, their presence meant that minority incumbents only needed to win over a relatively small minority of whites to triumph in the general election. Most minority incumbents redistricted into majority-white districts accomplished this goal with ease.

Democrats did not immediately benefit from the judicial shift against racial redistricting. The incumbency advantage allowed Republican incumbents to stave off defeat despite the presence of greater numbers of minority voters. In some cases, states had adopted plans specifically designed to preserve the racial and political balance of the congressional delegation despite the necessity of altering district boundaries. Democrats nevertheless gained hope of retaking some of these seats when they became open due to the narrow victories by some Republican incumbents in their initial election in the reconfigured districts.

Redistricting prior to the 2002 elections has largely preserved the status quo in terms of the number of majority-minority districts. Texas created only one new majority-Latino district despite pressures to create a second. Florida also created one new majority-Latino district. Like the other majority-Latino districts in Florida, this district will likely send a Cuban American Republican to the U.S. House. No southern state drew a new majority-black district. Most states drew the maximum feasible number of majority-black districts prior to the 1992 elections. *Shaw* and its progeny eliminated any districts unable to stand up to judicial scrutiny between 1992 and 2000. Consequently, it is difficult for states to construct new majority-black congressional districts able to withstand a racial gerrymandering lawsuit. On the other hand, some states have slightly increased the number of majority-black state legislative districts.

African Americans nonetheless gained one new seat in Georgia after the 2002 elections. Georgia Democrats adopted a highly partisan plan designed to increase the number of Democrats in the state's congressional delegation from three of eleven to seven of thirteen. The plan failed to work as intended due to a strong showing by Georgia Republicans in 2002, although the number of Democrats did increase to five of thirteen. All three of the existing congressional seats held by African American Democrats will continue to be occupied by black Democrats.

Additionally, African American David Scott won election from the 42 percent black Thirteenth District of Georgia. African Americans had also hoped to win the open 43 percent black Twelfth District. Though a black candidate was able to win the Democratic nomination in a runoff primary, he lost the general election to a Republican candidate in an upset. The black Democratic nominee had not held elected office in the past, although he was related to a powerful (but also controversial) state legislator.

Outside Georgia, African Americans made no further electoral gains in the South in 2002. Mapmakers have not created new majority-black districts or majority-white districts with sizeable minority populations likely to elect African Americans. Indeed, Virginia Republicans, who controlled the redistricting process in the Old Dominion, carefully reduced the African American population of the formerly 39 percent black Second District after African American State Senator Louise Lucas nearly won the district in the 2001 special election.

Outside Georgia and North Carolina, where they controlled the congressional redistricting process, Democrats found their opportunities for gains limited after the completion of the 2000 redistricting round. A variety of redistricting factors constrained the potential for Democratic gains. The necessity of maintaining existing majority-minority districts limited the ability of mapmakers to transfer Democratic voters into districts where they might swing the district against the GOP. The Republicans controlled or shared control of the redistricting process in some states to the detriment of Democratic efforts to draft pro-Democratic plans. In 2002, neither African Americans nor Democrats made substantial gains in the South at the congressional level; it remains to be seen if either group can gain many more seats during the remainder of the decade.

NOTES

1 Covered jurisdictions may also seek preclearance from the U.S. District Court of the District of Columbia. However, they have rarely pursued this option.

2 *Shaw v. Reno*. 509 U.S. 630 (1993).

3 Charles Cameron, David Epstein, and Sharyn O'Halloran, "Do Majority-Minority Districts Advance Black Substantive Representation in Congress?" *American Political Science Review* 90 (1996); Carol M. Swain, *Black Faces, Black Interests: The Representation of African Americans in Congress* (Cambridge, MA: Harvard University Press, 1995); Abigail Thernstrom, *Whose Votes Count? Affirmative Action and Minority Voting Rights* (Cambridge, MA: Harvard University Press, 1987). Of these three authors, only Cameron, Epstein, and O'Halloran undertook a systematic statistical analysis of the election of African Americans. None of these authors discusses Latino representation at any length.

4 Chandler Davidson and Bernard Grofman, eds., *Quiet Revolution in the South: The Impact of the Voting Rights Act 1965-1990* (Princeton, NJ: Princeton University Press, 1994); Bernard Grofman and Lisa Handley, "Minority Population and Black and Hispanic Congressional Success in the 1970s and 1980s," *American Politics Quarterly* 17 (October 1989):436-445; David Lublin, "The Election of African Americans and Latinos to the U.S. House of Representatives, 1972-1994," *American Politics Quarterly* 25 (1997a):269-286; David Lublin, *The Paradox of Representation: Racial Gerrymandering and Minority Interests in Congress* (Princeton, NJ: Princeton University Press, 1997): 39-52; Frank Parker, *Black Votes Count: Political Empowerment in Mississippi after 1965* (Chapel Hill, NC: University of North Carolina Press, 1990):136-143.

5 Grofman, Handley, and Lublin argue that realignment toward the Republicans may surprisingly aid the election of blacks under certain circumstances. Specifically, blacks need to compose a majority of Democratic primary electorate, and loyal Democrats need to form a majority in the general election; see Bernard Grofman, Lisa Handley, and David Lublin, "Drawing Effective Minority Districts: A Conceptual Framework and Some Empirical Evidence," *North Carolina Law Review* (2001).

6 Grofman and Handley, "Minority Population and Black and Hispanic Congressional Success"; Lublin, *The Paradox of Representation*, 45-48; Lublin, "The Election of African Americans and Latinos."

7 Cameron, Epstein, and O'Halloran, "Do Majority-Minority Districts Advance Black Substantive Representation," 805; Lublin, *The Paradox of Representation*, 99; David Lublin and D. Stephen Voss, "Racial Redistricting and Realignment in Southern State Legislatures," *American Journal of Political Science* 44 (4, October 2000):797-801.

8 Georgia drew two black districts in its original plan, but the Justice Department used its powers under Section 5 of the Voting Rights Act to block the plan from going into effect. Georgia then adopted a new plan with three black majority districts; see Robert A. Holmes, "Reapportionment Strategies in the 1990s: The Case of Georgia" in *Race and Redistricting in the 1990s*, edited by Bernard Grofman (New York: Agathon Press, 1998), 201-228.

9 Even the report by the NAACP Legal Defense Fund, which strongly argues that racial redistricting did not harm the Democrats, agrees that racial redistricting cost the Democrats three seats in Georgia in 1992. NAACP Legal Defense and Educational

Fund, "The Effect of Section 2 of the Voting Rights Act on the 1994 Congressional Elections," November 30, 1994. See David Lublin and D. Stephen Voss, "The Partisan Impact of Voting Rights Law: A Reply to Pamela S. Karlan," *Stanford Law Review* 50 (February 1998):765-778; and D. Stephen Voss and David Lublin, "Black Incumbents, White Districts: An Appraisal of the 1996 Congressional Elections," *American Politics Research* 29 (March 2001):141-182, for why dismantling two of the three black majority districts prior to the 1996 elections did not aid Democrats or result in the defeat of any black incumbents.

10 Lublin, *The Paradox of Representation*, 104-106.

11 Gingrich nearly lost the Republican primary in 1992.

12 Lublin and Voss, "The Partisan Impact of Voting Rights Law," 772-777.

13 I owe much to Lisa Handley's thoughts on this subject.

14 Lublin and Voss, "Racial Redistricting and Realignment in Southern State Legislatures," 801-803.

15 Cameron, Epstein, and O'Halloran, "Do Majority-Minority Districts Advance Black Substantive Representation," 805.

16 David Lublin, "The Real Story in Georgia," *Washington Post*, 27 August 2002, A15.

Table 7.1
Redistricting Losses from 1990 to 1994

	U.S. House			State House					
				Redistricting Losses					
	Number of New Black Districts	Number of Redistricting Losses	Gerrymander for the Democrats	Independent Effect	Interaction with Vote Swing	Total Redistricting Losses	Vote Swing Losses	Number of Seats	Number of New Black Districts
Alabama	1	2		1.8	0.9	2.7	3.3	105	7
Florida	3	2		7.2	1.9	9.1	1.9	120	4
Georgia	2	3		6.3	3.6	9.9	20.1	180	9
Louisiana	1	0	x	2.5	-0.3	2.2	-4.2	105	7
Mississippi	0	0		2.6	0.2	2.8	5.2	122	4
North Carolina	2	3	x	2.5	0	2.5	25.5	120	7
South Carolina	1	0		6.0	2.3	8.3	8.7	124	7
Tennessee	0	0		1.0	0.8	1.8	-3.8	99	1
Texas	1	0	x	1.2	2.2	3.4	-0.4	150	2
Virginia	1	-1	x	2.6	-0.3	2.3	3.7	100	3
Total	*12*	*9*	*4*	*33.7*	*11.3*	*45.0*	*60.0*	*1225*	*51*

Note: See David Lublin, *The Paradox of Representation* (Princeton, NJ: Princeton University Press, 1997); and David Lublin and D. Stephen Voss, "Racial Redistricting and Realignment in Southern State Legislatures," *American Journal of Political Science* 44:4, October 2000), 792–810, for information on how these numbers were estimated. A negative sign indicates a negative Democratic loss; in other words, the Democrats gained seats.

Table 7.2
Probability of a Democratic State House Victory by Black Percentage

	10%	20%	30%	40%	50%
Alabama	40	74	96	98	98
Arkansas	75	84	91	95	98
Florida	37	66	85	93	97
Georgia	31	56	78	90	96
Louisiana	48	72	87	94	97
Mississippi	39	49	72	89	96
North Carolina	20	63	94	99	100
South Carolina	0	35	45	97	100
Tennessee	77	80	76	96	100
Texas	18	65	92	98	100
Virginia	34	50	70	85	93

Note: See David Lublin and D. Stephen Voss, "Racial Redistricting and Realignment in Southern State Legislatures," *American Journal of Political Science* 44: 4 (October 2000), 792-810 for information on the estimation process. Estimates based on analysis of elections held in 1998 in all states except Louisiana, Mississippi, and Virginia. The Louisiana and Mississippi elections were held in 1995; the Virginia elections were held in 1997.

Table 7.3
Redistricting Impact on the Distribution of State Legislative and Congressional Districts, by Black Percentage

	<10%	10-20%	20-30%	30-40%	40-50%	50+%
Alabama	7	-2	-1	-8	-3	7
Florida	12	-4	-7	-3	-1	3
Georgia	6	6	-2	-8	-7	5
Louisiana	2	6	-1	-9	-5	7
Mississippi	-1	12	0	-8	-7	3
North Carolina	8	-3	-2	-10	1	6
South Carolina	7	-2	2	-6	-7	6
Tennessee	4	-3	-1	-1	0	1
Texas	8	-5	-3	0	-1	1
Virginia	6	-2	0	-3	-4	3
Congress	13	-1	-8	-14	-1	10

Note: Each cell in the table shows the change in the percentage of all seats that fell into that category of percent black under the districting plan used in the 1994 elections as compared to the plan used for the 1990 elections. For example, the "-7" in the third column for Florida means that the share of districts 20-30% black in 1994 decreased by 7% from 1990.

About the Authors

David A. Bositis

David Bositis is the senior political analyst at the Joint Center for Political and Economic Studies, where he also conducts polling. Formerly he was a professor at George Washington University and SUNY-Potsdam. Bositis began working on redistricting issues when the late Judge A. Leon Higgenbotham, Jr., representing the Congressional Black Caucus in the *Shaw* challenges of the early 1990s, asked him to write an expert witness report for *Hays v. Louisiana II.* He has been an expert witness in federal and state courts in Alabama (regarding the state's legislative map) and in Florida in *Johnson v. Mortham.* He is the author, coauthor, or editor of books and articles on political subjects, including *Redistricting and Representation: The Creation of Majority-Minority Districts and the Evolving Party System in the South* (Joint Center for Political and Economic Studies, 1995) and *Redistricting and Minority Representation: Learning from the Past and Preparing for the Future* (Joint Center for Political and Economic Studies, 1998). Bositis's research was cited by Justice Stevens in *Bush v. Vera* and in briefs in the North Carolina Easley case. He holds a B.A. from Northwestern University and an M.A. and Ph.D., both in political science, from Southern Illinois University.

Anita S. Earls

Anita S. Earls is director of advocacy at the University of North Carolina Center for Civil Rights. Currently she is representing plaintiffs in several voting rights cases that involve redistricting and ex-felon disenfranchisement. She served as a lead counsel for the plaintiffs in *NAACP v. Katherine Harris,* which challenged the disenfranchisement of Florida's black voters in the November 2000 elections. Formerly, Earls was director of the Voting Rights Project and coordinator of the Police Misconduct Initiative for the Lawyers Committee for Civil Rights Under Law. From 1988 to 2000, she served as deputy assistant attorney general in the Civil Rights Division of the U.S. Department of Justice, where she had responsibility for the division's Voting, Educational Opportunities, Disability Rights and Coordination and Review sections. Prior to that, Earls litigated civil rights cases as a partner with Ferguson, Stein, Wallas, Adkins, Gresham & Sumter in Charlotte, North Carolina. She is a graduate of Williams College and holds a law degree from Yale Law School, where she was a senior editor for the *Yale Law Journal.*

Leo F. Estrada

Leo Estrada is an associate professor of urban planning in the School of Public Policy and Social Research at UCLA. He also serves as the director of the North American Integration and Development Center at UCLA. His areas of expertise include ethnic and racial demographic trends, particularly of the Latino population in the U.S., inner city redevelopment, public policy analysis, and research methods. Estrada also serves on advisory boards to federal agencies, nonprofit organizations, hospitals, and foundations. He consults in the private sector and has served as an expert witness as well, including testimony on census undercount and redistricting issues. His earlier professional work includes academic positions at the University of North Texas, University of Texas at El Paso, and the University of Michigan at Ann Arbor, as well as two posts at the U.S. Bureau of the Census, where he was special assistant to the chief of the Population Division (1975-77) and staff assistant to the deputy director (1979-80). He holds a B.A. from Baylor University and an M.S. and Ph.D. from Florida State University.

Lisa Handley

Lisa Handley is a principal of Frontier International Electoral Consulting, a consulting firm that specializes in redistricting. She has advised numerous state and local jurisdictions, civil rights organizations, and the U.S. Department of Justice on redistricting and has served as an expert in dozens of redistricting and voting rights court cases over the past two decades. During the current (2000 Census) round of redistricting, she has advised more than a dozen states.

In addition to her work in the U.S., she has served as an international consultant on boundary delineation in emerging democracies and other election issues, working with such international organizations as the United Nations, the International Institute of Democracy and Electoral Assistance (IDEA), and the International Foundation for Election Systems (IFES). She has published numerous articles on redistricting and minority voting rights and is coauthor (with Bernard Grofman and Richard Niemi) of the book *Minority Representation and the Quest for Voting Equality* (Cambridge University Press, 1992). She has taught political science and methodology courses at the University of Virginia and George Washington University. She holds a Ph.D. in political science from George Washington University.

Bob Holmes

Bob Holmes is director of the Southern Center for Studies in Public Policy and professor of political science at Clark Atlanta University. In 2000, he was reelected to his fourteenth term as a state representative in the Georgia General Assembly, where he is a member of the Appropriations and Rules Committee and chairs the Governmental Affairs Committee. He has also served as chairman of the Georgia Legislative Black Caucus (1990-91). The author, coauthor, or editor of two dozen books and monographs, Holmes' writing on legislative politics and reapportionment/redistricting issues has appeared in notable academic journals, including *National Political Science Review*, *Phylon* and *Urban Research Review*, and in books such as *Black Politics and Black Political Behavior: A Linkage Analysis* (Hanes Walton, Jr., ed.; Greenwood, 1994), *Race and Redistricting in the 1990s* (Bernard Grofman, ed.; Agathon Press, 1998), and *Race and Representation* (Georgia Persons, ed.; Transaction Publishers, 1997). Holmes is also the editor of two annual publications, *Georgia Legislative Review* and *The Status of Black Atlanta.* He has served on the editorial advisory boards of the *Journal of Social and Behavioral Sciences*, *Phylon*, and *The Review of Black Political Economy.* He is a graduate of Shepherd College and holds a Ph.D. in political science from Columbia University.

David Lublin

David Lublin is associate professor of government at American University. Currently he is also the principal investigator on the Federal Elections Project, which is funded by the National Science Foundation. Lublin's expertise includes redistricting, an area for which he has served as an expert witness. His books include *The Paradox of Representation: Racial Gerrymandering and Minority Interests in the South* (Princeton University Press, 1997) and *The Republican South* (Princeton University Press, 2002). His articles on race and redistricting have appeared in the *American Political Science Review, American Journal of Political Science, Journal of Politics,* and *Stanford Law Review.* He has also written for the *Washington Post.* He holds a B.A. from Yale University and an M.A. and Ph.D. in government from Harvard University.

Laughlin McDonald

Since 1972, Laughlin McDonald has been director of the ACLU Southern Regional Office and Voting Rights Project in Atlanta. He is the author of *Racial Equality* (1977; re-released 1991 by NTC/Carolina Publishing); *The Rights of Racial Minorities: The Basic ACLU Guide to Racial Minority Rights* (Southern Illinois University Press, 1993); and *A Voting Rights Odyssey: Black Enfranchisement in Georgia* (Cambridge University Press 2003). McDonald has represented racial minorities in numerous voting and civil rights cases, and has testified frequently before Congress on voting rights issues. He has written extensively for both scholarly and popular publications on constitutional and civil liberties issues. He holds a B.A. and an L.L.B. from the University of Virginia.

www.ingramcontent.com/pod-product-compliance
Ingram Content Group UK Ltd.
Pitfield, Milton Keynes, MK11 3LW, UK
UKHW041104150926
475561UK00001BA/33

9 780761 830436